Born to Preach

Anne Gimenez

with

Robert Paul Lamb

Harrison House Publishers
Tulsa, Oklahoma

15 14 13 12 11   10 9 8 7 6 5 4 3 2 1

Born to Preach
Copyright © 2011 by Gimenez Evangelistic Association
P.O. Box 61777
Virginia Beach, VA 23466

Published by Harrison House
P.O. Box 35035
Tulsa, OK 74153
www.harrisonhouse.com

Printed in the United States of America.

Dedication

To everyone who has the call of God upon their lives and knows in their heart that they were born to preach.

There is no greater honor than to serve the Lord with your life. If you are willing to learn His ways, follow His voice and obey His Word, you can do whatever God has called you to do.

And I thank Christ Jesus our Lord who has enabled me, because He counted me faithful, putting me into the ministry.

1 Timothy 1:12 (NKJV)

Endorsements

If there ever was an appropriate title for a book about Anne Gimenez, *Born to Preach* would be it. And, the whole world has been blessed because of her life.

She and Brother John have ministered to us and our family for many, many years. Knowing them personally, watching their lives, and seeing Jesus manifest Himself in their work have been wonderful things—all these, and the best is yet to come.

Kenneth and Gloria Copeland

Anne Gimenez's *Born to Preach* is destined to be a classic for the generations to study and draw strength from in order to fulfill their God-given callings. "Sister Anne," as she is lovingly named by many who know her, has blazed a trail and opened the way for all believers to follow. Young emerging leaders, particularly women in leadership, will be strengthened by her resolve. I must admit that some of the trials she went through brought both a tear and a time of laughter as I recalled my own pioneer days. There isn't anything like this book! It isn't simply her memoirs, it is a roadmap for those who come after her to guide them in running the race for the high calling of Christ Jesus. Well done, my friend! I love this book!

Cindy Jacobs
Generals International

Born to Preach

Some young people think, *I'm just a teenager, how can God use me to change the world?* Anne's life story shows just how God raised this woman up to a higher calling than she ever imagined- and that's just what He wants to do with this next generation.

Ron Luce
President and Founder of Teen Mania Ministries

Bishop Anne Gimenez continues to amaze and inspire me with her love of the truth. She is not ashamed of the reality of Jesus Christ and the power of the Holy Ghost. Her book will be an inspiration to those who read it and is filled with revelation that can help any committed Christian to fulfill their destiny in God.

Bishop Wellington Boone

Answering the call to preach the Gospel is both an honor and a sacrifice. It is never easy but certainly always worth the price. To overcome all obstacles, beginning from birth, and still persevere in the faith is Anne Gimenez. What an example she is to the Body of Christ and what an encouragement *Born to Preach* will be to you. If you want to reach a higher level in your faith, stand on the shoulders of experience and grasp a touch of Heaven.

Dr. Marilyn Hickey
President, Marilyn Hickey Ministries

It has been my pleasure to know Anne Gimenez for decades! I know Anne to be a Godly, compassionate and anointed vessel of the Holy Spirit to proclaim the Gospel of Jesus Christ to America and the uttermost parts of the earth. You will enjoy her story.

Pastor John Hagee
Cornerstone Church, San Antonio, Texas

Acknowledgments

I want to sincerely thank everyone whose sacrifice and thoughtful help made this book possible.

First, I owe my deepest gratitude to the Lord Jesus Christ and my Heavenly Father. He alone has given me the grace to persevere through every valley and mountaintop experience, and has carried me all along the journey.

It is an honor for me to serve alongside great leaders in the Body of Christ who have inspired and encouraged me over the years. There are literally too many to cite all by name. However, I would like to point out the contributions of my Aunt Ruby Bailey, Garlon Pemberton, Oscar & Anna Salstrand, Pastor Harry Hodge, David & Lorraine Minor, Oral & Evelyn Roberts, John & Dodie Osteen, Freda Lindsay, Demos Shakarian, Pat & Dede Robertson, Bea Lamont, Lynn Lucas, my family, and so many others who affected my life.

I would like to thank Robert Paul Lamb for his masterful writing talent as a storyteller, and our superb editor, Sally Berk. I would also like to thank my son-in-law, John Blanchard, and Mary Strickland who assisted in the editorial work.

Furthermore, I am indebted to my elders, deacons, and church family at the Rock Church who supported me through this process. Also, I would like to show my gratitude to the ministers of the Rock Ministerial Fellowship for their faithfulness to the vision God has given our spiritual family.

I am especially grateful for the hard work of my daughter, Robin, who labored relentlessly to trust God for my healing from a near-fatal illness while we were in the midst of completing this project. And thank you to all the friends, family, and ministries that interceded fervently for my miraculous recovery. I would also like to acknowledge my granddaughter, Amelia, who is a great blessing and joy to my heart.

And last but not least, I am so very thankful to John Gimenez, who was an incomparable gift to me and to the world in his generation. I am looking forward to seeing him again on that glorious day at the eastern gate.

Anne Gimenez
Virginia Beach, VA

Table of Contents

Foreword

The call of God in a person's life is mysterious, without explanation or perceived merit. Yet, for those who fulfill the destiny that God has placed before them, there is a glorious fulfillment and ministry that is often without comprehension.

Imagine the sovereign work of God bringing together a young Texas girl and a Puerto Rican ex-heroin addict from the Bronx. Imagine the prejudice in Texas against "Braceros" or "wetbacks." Then imagine the sovereign work of God that brought a union for His glory out of what, in the natural, would seem an impossible combination. Anne Nethery from Texas married a member of a touring troupe of young Puerto Ricans from the Bronx called The Addicts. From that union came one of the fastest growing churches in America and a national event called "*Washington for Jesus*" that may well have changed the course of our nation's history.

But such is the calling of God in someone's life. Anne Gimenez has a call on her life. It has brought forth miracles and blessings to hundreds of thousands. Now, after decades of ministry, her dear husband, John Gimenez, has gone to be with the Lord. But Anne seems to go stronger than ever to fulfill the call that God placed on her life.

As I contemplate the life of these two people, I can only stand in amazement and say, "To God be the glory, great things He has done."

M. G. "Pat" Robertson
Chairman of the Board
The Christian Broadcasting Network, Inc.

Born to Preach

Introduction

When my long-time friend, Bishop Anne Gimenez called in June 2009 to talk about writing the biography of her life, she mentioned a prophetic word that had just been given a few weeks earlier at a Rock Church convention.

"Write, write, write...for there shall be a memory book that shall be written" was the prophetic word. "It will tell about the miracles and it will tell about the grace, and what you put down shall be for the next forty years for the generation that is to come..." She clearly believed it was a word from heaven to begin that task of writing the story heralded by the prophecy.

Although I had written another book, *Upon This Rock*, shortly before the first great Washington for Jesus rally in 1980, I discovered facets of Sister Anne's life that I never knew. Spared from an abortionist's knife and nurtured by her mother's sisters whose lives had been impacted by the miraculous works of God springing from Azusa Street, she emerged as a singular-minded, fiery, finger-pointing evangelist in a day when few women embraced that role. Some of the stories we've told in this new book about her life are the kinds of testimonies that will long be repeated.

Her marriage to former drug addict John Gimenez wasn't given much chance at success—even by close friends. Yet, their marriage not only succeeded, they became a powerful husband-wife team impacting the nation through television and the massive Washington for Jesus rallies in the 1980s and 1990s.

Born to Preach

Of all the things I appreciate about Sister Anne, there is one that stands out above the rest. Once she's heard a word from God on a matter, she—and her late husband, John—were *completely* fearless to follow it. They were not deterred. That's not only been the story of how Rock Church was birthed, but how this woman of God came from obscurity into great usefulness in God's kingdom. Although she and I have worked on other projects before, I must admit this one is my favorite. And I am particularly grateful to God for her miraculous recovery from near-death in 2010 while this project was still underway.

Born to Preach comes covered in prayer that it might bless, encourage and strengthen every person who reads it, and particularly, those who choose to follow the principles Anne Gimenez has lived. This woman of God is a treasured gift to the Body of Christ.

Robert Paul Lamb

Co-Author

Chapter 1

"Get Rid of This Child"

Anne and her sister Beverly Jean

Born to Preach

Chapter 1

"Get Rid of This Child"

"If abortions had been legal in the 1930s, I have no doubt I would have never—ever—seen the light of day."

—*Anne Gimenez*

"I want you to get rid of this child!"

Those were my overwhelmed father's words to my mother who was then three months pregnant with me, her second child.

Mother could hardly believe her ears. Had her husband just asked her to kill their baby? "I will not give up this child!" Mother exclaimed, tears gathering in her eyes. "I'll not do such a thing… no matter what! I *want* this baby."

"Pauline, there's no other way," he countered, barely controlling his rage.

"You're just upset because there's no work," Mother replied softly. "I believe Jesus will make a way for us…"

"Jesus? What's *He* got to do with it?"

"He'll make a way…He always has," she continued. "Besides, I'll never kill my baby."

"It *has* to be done," he insisted.

My parents, Charles Saben Nethery and Ina Pauline Adams, had met and married in Houston, Texas, as smitten teenagers on the last day of June 1928, as the nation stood unknowingly on the verge of the Great Depression. My only sister, Beverly Jean, came along in January 1931.

The Depression had hit Texas with a vengeance. Gone was the prosperity the state had experienced during the "oil booms" near Beaumont in the early 1900s and the 1920s. By 1932, many people from all walks of life had lost their jobs, and my father was one of them.

❧ ❧

Daddy had not had an easy life. His birth mother had died when he was only four, and he was raised by an abusive step-mother. His father worked for the railroad and was absent for long stretches at a time. He continually ran away from home over the mistreatment. Finally, he left for good in his early teens and never returned.

Growing up, Daddy had learned nothing of the Word of God or of taking a stand of faith for his family. Now, with no visible means of support, and another child on the way, he was over-whelmed. Without faith in God and newly unemployed, he saw no problem with an abortion—legal or not. He did not want another mouth to feed and was looking for a way out. I'm sure he felt trapped and did not know where to turn.

Mother, on the other hand, was raised to know and serve the Lord Jesus. Life was precious to her, especially her unborn baby's life. Her natural instincts as a mother was to love, nurture, and protect her baby, no matter what.

Yet, her husband—the man she promised to love, cherish, and obey—was absolutely determined this baby must not live! What could she do?

Reeling from her husband's demand, Mother locked herself in a closet and cried out to God. Afterward, she could never remember how long she remained in that tiny cubicle, but before she left it, God gloriously filled her with His Holy Spirit. Her life would never be the same again.

That very day, God placed His shield of protection over my life—sparing me from the abortionist's knife—and called me His own. When I arrived 22 months after my sister, on the morning of November 26, I was marked to be a vessel of God.

It took a miracle to get me here, and my arrival marked the beginning of a life of miracles—a life that has kept me ever so close to the Miracle Maker.

Born to Preach

Chapter 2

This Is My Story

Anne and her sister playing dolls

Born to Preach

Chapter 2

This Is My Story

"This is my story, this is my song, praising my Savior all the day long."

—from "Blessed Assurance" by Fannie Crosby

My story begins in Houston, Texas, named after Sam Houston, the famed hero of the Texas War of Independence.

Until 1901, Houston was a sleepy town on the state's southeast coast. Then, oil was discovered in nearby Beaumont, and the area began its transformation into a thriving metropolis. The Great Depression slowed the process somewhat, but by 1939, when I was seven years old, Houston had become the most populous city in Texas.

Since the beginnings of the 20th century, Houston has always been a significant location in Pentecostal circles. It was there in 1905 when Charles Fox Parham, a former Methodist pastor, who embraced the Spirit-filled experience several years earlier, launched a Bible school, and became the mentor of William J. Seymour.

Born to Preach

A year later, Seymour took the Pentecostal message to Los Angeles, spawning a three-year "Azusa Street" revival that would ultimately affect the lives of hundreds of millions around the world.

Shortly before the U.S. entered into World War I, Eli Noble Richey was called to Houston to pastor a declining church known as Gospel Tabernacle. Pastor Richey had been influenced in the 1890s by Alexander Dowie's ministry of divine healing. He had a large family including eight children, who all devoted their lives to the ministry. The family, together with the youngest son, Raymond T. Richey, all moved to Houston to work with their parents.

Spurred by the growth of an Army base and an air field, Houston's population grew, and so did the work of Houston Evangelistic Temple, as it was now called. Within eight years, the congregation had mushroomed from fifty or sixty to some two thousand and had multiple outreaches to the community.

In the early 1920s, working with his family, Raymond T. Richey became widely known as a "healing evangelist," as he took the Pentecostal truths throughout the nation. The Richeys' meetings were characterized by incredible miracles of healing, deliverance and salvation of souls. By 1925, it was estimated that over 100,000 had committed themselves to Christ in a three-year period and tens of thousands were healed of their infirmities and diseases.

After one revival meeting, a parade was held for those who had been healed. It was thirteen blocks long. In another meeting in Tulsa, Oklahoma, there were 11,000 conversions, and so many people were healed of crippling diseases that a pick-up truck was piled high with crutches and other medical devices left behind.

During this time, my maternal grandparents—Agnes and Joseph Adams—were members of a Nazarene church that exposed them to holiness teaching. When Joseph passed away unexpectedly at age 45, Agnes, a devout believer, was left to raise her six children alone. She did so, selflessly.

When her oldest daughter, Myrtle, was dying at age nineteen of tuberculosis, then known as the "white plague," a friend told the family about a tent meeting where a woman preacher was praying for the sick. They took Aunt Myrtle to the meeting, and she received a miracle of healing and was gloriously filled with the Holy Spirit.

Because of my aunt's miraculous healing, my grandmother, all four daughters, and both sons became Pentecostal believers. The woman preacher who conducted the tent meeting may have been Maria Woodworth-Etter, whose ministry reads like a page taken from the book of Acts. That single miracle shaped and influenced multiple generations of my family's history.

❦

When I was six months old, Mother and her sisters took me with them to a service at the Houston Evangelistic Temple, where Raymond T. Richey's father, Eli "Dad" Richey, was still the pastor. That day, babies were being dedicated, but my mother was too shy to take me down front. Instead, my Aunt Ruby took me to the altar, where "Dad" Richey took me in his arms and prayed a simple prayer of dedication, setting me apart as a vessel of God.

Born to Preach

As Beverly and I grew up, Mother occasionally took us to Sunday night services at the old Tabernacle off Capitol Avenue. To get there, we had to take a bus. The three of us would stand on the street corner, sometimes in the biting cold, waiting on the right bus to take us across town. When we would finally arrive, I loved to sit under the anointed atmosphere in that lively church with the fiery preaching and the happy singing.

Throughout my childhood, Aunt Ruby Bailey continued to influence my spiritual development. She and Uncle Louie lived on a ranch outside Channelview, Texas, about ten miles east of Houston.

The Baileys attended a little Assembly of God Church, pastored, at that time, by William Bythel Hagee. One of his sons, John Hagee, later became a well-known pastor and television preacher in San Antonio.

Aunt Ruby saw to it that Beverly and I stayed with her and Uncle Louie two weeks in the summertime, so we could attend Vacation Bible School. Attending that VBS was, in fact, the only religious training I received as a child. My father refused to allow Beverly and me to go to church and was furious if he ever found we'd actually attended a service somewhere. He always claimed to be a Methodist, but there was little evidence of that claim. When Beverly and I stayed at our aunt and uncle's, however, he had no say in the matter.

My earliest encounter with God came at the age of twelve, when my parents were having serious marital problems and talking about divorce. Daddy continually belittled my mother, even though she earnestly tried to please him. Today, we'd certainly call her an abused woman. Being the youngest, I was terribly distraught with what might happen to my sister and me if our parents were to separate.

One night, I was in the tub taking a bath and thinking about a terrible incident that had occurred in the house the evening before. A sense of needing to be right with God overwhelmed my soul and I began praying aloud, with tears flowing.

"Oh, Lord, please take care of us," I sobbed. I knew God *could* answer my prayer, but I wondered if He *would*. I wasn't serving Him as I should, but in my heart I knew I needed Him.

When I learned that my father hadn't wanted me, I was devastated. Knowing that he had tried to convince Mother to abort me tortured my heart. Besides, I believed he loved Beverly more. One day I'd overheard him telling her, "You're my favorite."

So, growing up, I felt unworthy and unloved. Beverly was always pretty and had lots of friends. I was quiet and shy and all too frequently in trouble with my father about something.

Beverly often teased me about my shyness. "What kind of girl are you?" she asked one day. "You can't even hold your head up when I introduce you."

Daddy's world centered on his work as an announcer at radio station KXYZ in Houston. He gave the daily news reports and regularly served as the announcer at local concerts and variety shows. Occasionally, he even got to introduce such famous personalities as Perry Como, Tyrone Power, Henry Fonda and Clark Gable.

When his job required it, he could also be courageous. Once, in order to report on an incoming hurricane, he tied himself to an antenna atop a multi-storied building in downtown Houston. The stunt drew widespread attention.

Born to Preach

&capprox;

In 1945, my father and mother were finally divorced, and Daddy moved to Corpus Christi to work with Gulf Coast Broadcasting and launch the first NBC affiliate radio station there. Beverly and I remained in Houston with our mother, and my Aunt Velma and her daughter Patsy came to live with us in a house at the corner of College and Northwestern Streets.

Without Daddy around, the little two-bedroom, wood frame house was peaceful. We had no car, so we had to take a bus to get anywhere, including the grocery store and the services we attended across town at Evangelistic Temple.

My best friend at this time was a girl named Beverly Casey. She and I would save our money until we had enough to buy a pack of Lucky Strike cigarettes at the corner drugstore. When we'd go to the movies, we'd bring those "Luckies" out and smoke them. It was about the most sinful thing we ever did, but it made us feel grownup.

During summer vacations, my sister, Beverly, and I visited our father in Corpus Christi. In June of 1948, he and Mother were remarried with only a week's notice for Beverly and me; this event immediately took a toll on my young life. Four months later, in October, we moved from Houston to Corpus Christi and into a two-bedroom apartment on 18th Street across from the junior college. I had to deal with the stress of changing schools in my senior year and with the even greater strain of having Daddy back living with us again.

The summers Beverly and I spent with Aunt Ruby and Uncle Louie on their farm in Channelview were always an escape for me.

Chapter 2: This Is My Story

Together, the Baileys made me feel loved and special, treating me like one of their own children. And I loved life on the farm.

Tall and lanky, Uncle Louie always wore boots and a ten gallon hat. He worked for an oil refinery and loved riding horses and herding cattle. Aunt Ruby was a soft-spoken homemaker who excelled in cooking, canning, gardening and sewing. The visits were made even more special when my grandmother moved there. She showered me with attention, teaching me Bible stories and sewing dresses out of feed sacks.

Even with my regular visits to Channelview, though, it wasn't until I was sixteen that I made a lasting commitment to serve God with all of my heart.

By then, in the spring of 1949, I already had a boyfriend whom I'd met on a blind date to go horseback riding. Five years older and handsome, Waymond Dugger was already in college. He was nearly six feet tall and looked like a cowboy with his boots and wrinkled Stetson. Surprisingly, my family liked him. We enjoyed each other's company and even attended church services together.

Later that year, when I contracted a mysterious illness, doctors gave me penicillin, at first suspecting an infection in my chest but later dismissed that possibility. I was sick for several weeks, and the pain was unremitting.

Beverly came into my bedroom one day and announced, "I heard about a tent meeting over by the college where they're praying for the sick. You ought to go over there and get prayed for."

I knew about divine healing because my grandmother had told me continually about my aunt being healed of tuberculosis.

Born to Preach

I wondered—could that really happen to me? So far, nothing was helping me—even the doctors had no answers. I was desperate.

It was now October, 1949. The tent meeting Beverly told me about was being held by T.L. and Daisy Osborn and Gordon and Freda Lindsay—two unassuming couples who would one day touch millions of lives. They literally impacted the destiny of nations in their lifetimes. My life, too, was about to change radically.

I asked Waymond to take me to the meeting on a Friday night. Our church attendance had been more social in times past; we would go to church because that is what "nice" people did. But there was something very different about this service. It was alive and Spirit-filled, just like Evangelistic Temple. I was in the crosshairs of a divine encounter.

I didn't know it at the time, but our attendance at this service would signal the beginning of a shift in our relationship. We went to the revival that night, but Waymond was not moved like I was. From then on, he would remain the same, but my priorities would begin to change. My destiny was calling.

❧❦

The next afternoon, I was compelled to go back to the tent meeting with another hundred people or so. This time I went alone. Freda Lindsay was speaking on being filled with the Holy Ghost, and it sounded so simple and easy. At the end of the message, she asked those who wanted to receive the baptism of the Holy Spirit to stand to their feet.

To my surprise, I was on my feet instantly. Along with the others, I went back to the prayer tent. Kneeling in the sawdust, I tried to pray but was soon distracted and started to leave.

Just then, a still, small Voice stopped me. *You haven't done what the preacher told you to do,* the Voice said. *If you get into My presence, you will receive.*

Back on my knees, I lifted my hands and began to worship the Lord. I had gone to the meeting for a healing, but God had something far more important for me that day. I prayed, "Lord, this is so good, it doesn't even matter if you heal me or not!" That's when I heard someone speaking in other tongues, but I wasn't going to let it bother me. I had heard that kind of praying at my aunt's Pentecostal church. But I thought you had to practically *be* in heaven to receive that gift. Then to my utter surprise, I realized—it was me!

Walking back home I felt like I was three feet off the ground. "Guess what?" I said to my mother as I came through the front door.

She stopped and stared at me for a moment, and then big tears filled her eyes and rolled down her cheeks. "You've got the Holy Ghost," she replied, smiling.

Mother had recognized God's presence upon me. I just knew I felt different. But in time, I learned the Holy Spirit had come to live within me, bringing a unique work of grace in preparation for the journey God had for my life.

The next day, I walked back to the tent for the afternoon service to get my healing. T.L. Osborn was preaching and praying for the sick. "We're going to pray for you, but you must understand that you are healed by the stripes laid upon the back of Jesus," he preached.

Born to Preach

I stepped into the prayer line, believed that I would be healed and was touched by the Healer. The painful symptoms came back later that day, but I persisted believing God had healed me. The next day as I confessed my healing, the pain lessened. By the third day, all of the pain was gone.

Those two encounters changed the course of my life. I had met Jesus the Savior as Healer and Baptizer—*all by myself.* No one could ever be the same again after such an experience—not even a shy teenage girl who lived in Corpus Christi, Texas.

The next day, Sunday, something unexpected happened that would plant me in the church that would change the course of my life. Waymond and I planned to attend the Baptist church on Alameda Street, where Pastor Lester Roloff was preaching. He was widely-known as an independent fundamentalist Baptist preacher who preached over the radio against a host of evils, including television and psychology.

Then, my father got wind of our plans. "I'll not have you attending a church where that fanatic is speaking," he fumed.

The prospect of my going to that Baptist church so filled him with rage that I thought he was going to hit me. Waymond and I quickly agreed we wouldn't embarrass him by going to hear Pastor Roloff.

"I know another place down here on Elizabeth and Alameda called the Corpus Christi Tabernacle," I suggested to Waymond as we left. "Let's go there."

When we arrived at the meeting, several hundred worshipers were already gathered inside the long, narrow frame building and were seated in its dark wooden pews. Upon entering the church, I immediately liked its spirited atmosphere. The singing was lively, and the preaching strong and forceful. It was like Aunt Ruby's church.

As I sat listening to Pastor Garlon Pemberton preach on the grace of God, I had difficulty focusing. I could not help but think how difficult life had been since my father had come home. His aggression toward my new faith had left me feeling somewhat shaken.

"If you really need the grace of God in your life today, raise your hand," the pastor said. My boyfriend was sitting on my right side, so I raised my left hand, hoping he couldn't see me.

"If you really want the grace of God, I want you to stand up," the pastor preached.

I suddenly found myself standing up.

But the pastor didn't stop there. "If you *really* want this grace in your life, I want you to come to the front and put your nose in this carpet and ask God for this grace," he enthused.

I was so far out of the boat by then, I had no other choice than to go forward. I felt as though I could not resist that altar call. It was almost as if I was being pulled out of my seat. I walked to the front and went to my knees asking God for that special grace I needed to live for Him. Tears streamed down my face. It was a moment I would never forget.

In June of 1950, I graduated from high school and later that summer, Waymond was drafted into the Army and wound up in Korea. Before he left, however, I made an announcement he was not expecting.

Waymond and I were sitting in my living room talking with my mother about our dreams for the future. I had always thought he and I would marry one day, but I was also becoming convinced of my calling.

"Don't laugh at me," I announced, "because I want to tell you something."

"What?" he asked.

"One of these days," I began slowly. "I can't tell you how or when, but I'm going to preach the Gospel of Jesus Christ."

"Really?" he said, sounding surprised.

"Yeah," I continued. "I may be old and gray when it happens but I know I'll preach one of these days."

It was the first time I had ever verbalized anything about my life's purpose. I had always been so shy and withdrawn, and it was not easy for me to express myself at times.

I had known that I would preach ever since I was a little girl, but now I had actually spoken aloud about God's calling. How the Almighty would ever cause it to happen, I did not know. But that summer, He began to show me what He had in mind for me.

❧

During my teen years (I was now 18), my Aunt Myrtle, Mother's oldest sister, was a strong influence in my life. A vivacious, outgoing person, she lived in Dallas. She had married a former mayor of Garland, Texas, and was herself an ordained minister. Jovial Aunt Myrtle always seemed to know where revival meetings were happening in the area.

In the summer of 1950, Aunt Myrtle and I attended a large "camp meeting," a tent revival, in Herman Park in downtown Houston, where Myrtle "Mom" Beale, one of the Pentecostal pioneers from Detroit and founder of Bethesda Missionary Temple, had come to preach.

The Bethesda church was one of the revival centers from the Latter Rain Movement that had begun in February 1948 at a Bible school in Canada. Now, the movement was spreading across America, with many people experiencing the signs, wonders, and a renewal of the gifts of the Holy Spirit.

Aunt Myrtle also took me to the big tent meetings between Ft. Worth and Dallas, where the great healing evangelists of the day came—Oral Roberts, Jack Coe, A.A. Allen, David Nunn, W.V. Grant, A.C. Valdez Jr. and O.L. Jaggers.

In one of these meetings, O.L. Jaggers announced, "The Lord told me He was going to heal blind eyes today. So, if you're blind, I want you to come right up here."

I watched with awe in my heart as several people went forward, were prayed over, and went back to their seats seeing. But one young man had been born without an eyeball. The evangelist had ten people come forward to confirm the young man had no eyeball.

Jaggers then had the young man sit on the platform as he preached out of the first chapter of Ephesians. The words were electric:

Blessed be the God and Father of our Lord Jesus Christ, who has blessed us with every spiritual blessing in the heavenly places in Christ, just as He chose us in Him before the foundation of the world…

In Him also we have obtained an inheritance, being predestined according to the purpose of Him who works all things according to the counsel of His will, that we who first trusted in Christ should be to the praise of His glory...

...the eyes of your understanding being enlightened; that you may know what is the hope of His calling, what are the riches of the glory of His inheritance in the saints, and what is the exceeding greatness of His power toward us who believe...

Ephesians 1:3-4; 11-12; 18-19 NKJV

The message was so stirring that people stood and shouted as the evangelist preached. The atmosphere was charged with faith in God. When Jaggers finished his message, he asked the young man to come forward and questioned if he was seeing yet. The answer was no. He prayed over the young man but there was still no result.

About the third time Jaggers prayed, the young man said "I see spots of light." The preacher prayed again, and this time he said, "I see poles and lines." Jaggers had about twenty people come forward, who testified they saw an eyeball forming in an empty socket! The young man received his sight that night.

As I witnessed the acts of God happening in those unforgettable tent services, I began to think, *One of these days I'll be doing the same thing. I know it will happen.*

Chapter 3

Ordained

Anne at 19

Born to Preach

Chapter 3

Ordained

"Before I formed you in the womb I knew [and] approved of you [as My chosen instrument], and before you were born I separated and set you apart, consecrating you; [and] I appointed you as a prophet to the nations."

—Jeremiah 1:5 (Amplified Bible)

One Sunday my sister, Beverly, and I went to a service at the Tabernacle and learned that there was to be a "presbytery" that day. That meant the church's pastor, Garlon Pemberton, his brother, Modest, and another minister would be laying hands on people and giving them prophetic words about the calling of God upon their lives.

Although the "presbyters" did not know me, I was called to the altar and Pastor Pemberton began to prophesy over me. The prophetic words were stunningly accurate, reflecting the deepest desires of my heart.

"Yea, My child…thou art a chosen vessel, chosen all the days of thy life. Thou art a peculiar treasure, even in thy home thou art noted as such…

Born to Preach

"The Lord has reserved thee for this last revival...He has poured out His Spirit mightily on thee. Thou were chosen as a little girl, yea chosen all thy life...

"The Lord doth lead thee and go before thee. Thou shalt walk in His footsteps and hear Him say, 'This is the way. Walk ye therein...'"

Before we left church that day, Pastor Garlon, a friendly, dark-haired man, came to me and asked, "Did you know you were called to preach?"

"Yes, sir," I answered.

"How long have you known?" he inquired.

"As long as I can remember," I said.

That service was a defining moment for me. I had known that I was called, but now a *desire* to preach came into my life. That desire to preach God's Word took root and began to grow in my heart. I had a fresh expectation that God's plan for my life was beginning to unfold in a new way.

Several months later, the Pembertons left to pastor another church in Houston. Oscar Salstrand and his wife, Anna, both graduates of Life Bible College in California, came to lead the congregation in Corpus Christi.

One Sunday morning, Pastor Salstrand surprised me by asking if I would lead the worship service. The church had been briefly without a worship leader since the previous one moved to Alice, Texas, to pastor. And now, nobody else seemed to want the job.

As I stepped into that role, though unsure of myself, I quickly discovered I had a good sense of rhythm and could keep time with the music, using the tambourine with ease. Much to my surprise, I actually enjoyed the position.

Chapter 3: Ordained

I was asked to lead the singing several more times, and each time, I agreed, thinking I'd handle the job until somebody else came along. Nobody else did, and I continued to lead the worship service as long as I attended the church—some fifteen years! Looking back, I see how God used that position to train me; it was there that I learned to be at ease standing before an audience and leading the worship. I learned firsthand how to speak publically, to pray without inhibitions, and to prophesy. The Lord was equipping me for what was to come.

❧

Having graduated from high school at seventeen, I got a job and resolved to one day marry Waymond. Having a boyfriend obviously filled a need in my life. I truly thought I was in love, and my family even affirmed my choice.

But something had happened after I received the infilling of the Holy Spirit. The more I became involved with the things of God, the less I was interested in a boyfriend. However, I was not entirely ready to end the relationship, either.

One day, I found myself in a place praying to God about my life. "I'll give up anything for You, Lord," I prayed, and then I took a deep breath. "Anything but Waymond…please don't make me give him up."

We had been dating now for several years, and Waymond wanted to get married. He became even more interested in finalizing plans after learning he was being drafted to serve in the Korean War. But I knew in my heart I could never marry someone who didn't have the same commitment to Jesus that I did. I had now been in church over a year and had learned the Scripture about being unequally yoked.

Born to Preach

When Waymond came back from Korea, we both had changed and our relationship was never the same. He was different from his overseas experiences, and I was decidedly changed by the Holy Spirit. Whatever threads that had held us together before, now unraveled, and we soon parted company.

Even though I missed him, I sensed I was being separated unto God for a purpose. At times, I felt isolated, with no one really to talk to about the breakup with Waymond, or about my sense that I was being kept for God's purpose. Other than my aunts' family, I had never been around people who talked about the Lord.

Growing up, I had learned not to confide in my mother. On several occasions, she had shared the private things I told her with my father, who then would throw my words back in my face. Each time that happened, I felt betrayed.

⚬⚬⚬

Outside of work and home, I became involved with the group of young people at the Tabernacle. On weekends, I took part in the street meetings and jail services they held. Besides Corpus Christi, we held meetings in nearby towns like Sinton, Kingsville, Refugio, Aransas Pass, and Ingleside.

The Tabernacle in Corpus Christi held a "family" connection to the Houston Evangelistic Temple, where "Dad" Richey had dedicated me as a baby. His son, evangelist Raymond T. Richey, had founded the Sabine Tabernacle in Beaumont, Texas, and they were affiliated with the Corpus Christi Tabernacle that I attended.

In 1932, Brother Richey turned the small Sabine Tabernacle congregation over to an exceptionally gifted man of God, Pastor

Chapter 3: Ordained

Harry Hodge. He had inherited an unfinished building on a small strip of land in Beaumont, and within a matter of years, had built a facility seating nearly two thousand people. The church held two services daily and three on Sunday for over twenty-two years.

Stories were often told about unusual revivals occurring under Brother Hodge's ministry. One such revival in 1937 was nicknamed "The Call" and eventually resulted in the church owning an entire city block.

Taking a cue from the Old Testament book of Joshua, the congregation marched around the block at 2 a.m. for six consecutive days, with Brother Hodge leading them. On the seventh day they marched around the block seven times.

Dogs running loose in the neighborhood could have been a danger, but the marchers claimed the passage in Exodus 11:7, which says that a dog shall not move his tongue at any man. The animals ran up to the marchers, but amazingly, not one of them barked.

As time passed, parcels of land surrounding the church came on the market and were purchased until the entire city block was in the hands of God's people. It had all happened through simple acts of faith and obedience.

Pastor Hodge's life-changing ministry was legendary among Pentecostal and Full Gospel believers throughout Texas, Oklahoma, and Louisiana, where he had pioneered numerous churches. He had traveled and preached throughout the country and overseas, ministering in churches like the famed Angelus Temple in Los Angeles, where Aimee Semple McPherson was pastor.

I was first introduced to Brother Hodge through a daily quarter-hour radio program which I listened to while getting ready for school. One day, my pastor told me Brother Hodge was coming to the Tabernacle to ordain some people.

"Wouldn't you like to be ordained?" he asked.

I didn't have to think twice. If there was anybody I would have wanted to be ordained by, it was Harry Hodge. "Yes," I said immediately.

Brother Hodge was a heavy-set man who resembled a well-dressed banker. He preached the message at the next Sunday service, and when he closed, the ordination candidates—including me—knelt down to be prayed over. It was March 9, 1951.

For years to come, I would cherish the memory of being ordained by this gifted man of God, who had licensed and ordained hundreds of ministers over the years, and in whose life all the gifts of the Spirit operated. When he laid hands upon someone, results always followed.

Soon after that event, I was given my first opportunity to preach—for the Friday night youth service at the Tabernacle. I had no idea how to prepare a message, but I knew the first step was to pray.

But the more I prayed, the more scared I became. One night I even dreamed I got up to speak and couldn't utter a sound. I was so stressed over the prospect, I even considered canceling. I literally didn't know what to do.

Then, God spoke to my heart, *Watch and pray that another does not take your crown.*

What did that mean? I pondered.

Chapter 3: Ordained

The answer came back quickly. *Someone is going to preach Friday. It doesn't have to be you, but don't let another take your crown.*

Now, I was afraid *not* to preach. It seemed the Lord was saying, "This is your time. Don't let someone else take it from you." So, I shoved all of my reserve and hesitation aside.

I decided to preach what I knew—and that was, Jesus saved me—so I strode boldly up to the pulpit and delivered my very first message!

At the next Sunday morning service after my debut, Brother Salstrand observed, "Sister Anne preached for us Friday night. She told us everything she knew and a lot of things she *didn't know!*" I was the mouthpiece, but truly, I knew that the Lord had spoken through me!

One Sunday night, I was scheduled to preach in Alice, Texas, and by Sunday afternoon, I still had received no leading about what to preach. When I left Corpus, taking a carload of young people with me, I still didn't have a message. Inwardly, I cried out to God for help.

As we drove along, the Lord began speaking to me. *I didn't tell you to decide the menu,* He said. *I only told you to dish it out.*

I had wanted some kind of power-packed evangelistic message, but the only message I had been given was on peace—so that's exactly what I preached.

At the close of the service, nearly everyone in the church was on their faces at the altar. I came to understand God always knew best what each church needed to hear. I just needed to be faithful in preaching the message I had been given.

Born to Preach

❦

Eventually, I became leader of the church youth group and spoke most Friday nights. One night after the youth service, I saw two young men coming down the aisle—heading directly towards me. I knew Brother Rollof had a school in town training preachers in his strict fundamentalist beliefs and I suspected these two were part of that school.

One of them looked me in the eye, and in a tone of authority, said, "As a woman, you are not supposed to be preaching."

"Really?" I questioned.

For several minutes, they absolutely hammered me with scripture after scripture about the wrongness of being a woman and preaching. Inwardly, I was saying "Lord, I don't know what to say to these people." No one had ever confronted me in that way before.

After they finished, I took a deep breath and calmly replied, "You certainly have a right to your opinion, but one of these days I'll stand before God and give an account of what I did with the calling upon my life."

"So what does that mean?" one of the men retorted with a smug look.

"It means I'll answer to God one day but I will never answer to you," I concluded.

"Well then, can you tell me by what authority are you preaching?" they continued to grill me.

"I am anointed," I said firmly.

Chapter 3: Ordained

I had served in a local church as a Sunday School teacher, a youth leader and a worship leader; nobody had ever challenged me in any of those roles. It never dawned on me that whole segments of the body of Christ had disqualified women from certain jobs in the church based solely on their gender. I would continue to hear some of these arguments for years to come.

❧☙

In addition to my role in the local church, I worked full time in the accounting department of a large petroleum company. And, because I still lived at home with my parents, I was constantly dealing with deeply upsetting family matters.

By this time, we had moved out to the southwestern part of Corpus, past the new Ray High School, and my parents had bought a new two-bedroom frame house at 813 Anderson Street.

From the time I had graduated from high school at age 17, I had paid room and board to my parents and, for the most part, they treated me as a "boarder" instead of their daughter.

But one day, I came home for lunch and opened a can of tomato soup. It might have cost ten cents. Later, my mother told my father what I had done and he angrily confronted me. "What you're paying for in room and board didn't cover the cost of that soup," he snapped.

"As long as you live here," he told me, "you're not to do that again. It's not yours to do with."

His hurtful words cut me to the core. I thought his anger had something to do with Beverly, but she was married and living elsewhere now. Yet his anger continued. The trouble over a can of tomato soup foreshadowed an even more volatile confrontation to come.

I just kept busy. Each weekend, the Tabernacle held street meetings or youth services in small towns near Corpus, often using a city park for the venue. Sometimes we went to the city jail and held services. In addition, the church sponsored a radio program and I preached regularly over the air waves.

My father's broadcast career continued to advance. He helped launch KRIS-TV in 1956—the first full-power NBC affiliate in South Texas—and ultimately rose to become vice president of the company. As a result of his media jobs, he became known quite well as an "on air" personality, and I knew sooner or later he would find out about my preaching activities.

One night after supper, I felt he needed to hear of my evangelism work from me instead of somebody else. Even though I could never seem to talk to him about a problem without causing an explosion, I thought I'd make the effort.

When he learned what I was doing—preaching on the streets and on the radio, he went livid. His face turned red and he stood up from his living room chair, seething, and ordered me to leave the house.

"You've humiliated me," he shouted, "and I'll probably lose my job now. Will you be able to support me if that happens?" He told me I had to leave.

Stunned, I just stood there for a moment. I could not believe what I was hearing. I wasn't living a life of immorality or debauchery. I was just following my calling in life. But dutifully, I picked up the keys to my '41 Ford Cooper, grabbed my purse and walked out into the warm night air.

My father stood in the doorway and called after me in the darkness: "You don't ever need to come back to this house again."

With nowhere else to go, I spent that night with my best friend in the church, Bobbie Newland. I called my mother several days later to see if I could come over and wash my clothes. I didn't know how to run a washing machine. She answered, "When you left home, you forfeited all of your rights." I realized that I would have to be more independent than what I'd counted on.

I was utterly shut out by my parents, the ones who were supposed to care for me more than anyone in the world. Yet, I found that anyone who ever pushed me off always pushed me closer to God—there was nowhere else to turn.

Bobbie and her husband, Rod, graciously opened their home to me. They lived next door to the Tabernacle, and I rented a room from them for the next eighteen months.

Bobbie came from a background of deep sin and had been miraculously converted. A fiery preacher in her own right, she had a genuine calling in prophetic ministry, and we had often talked about doing team ministry together—a common practice in the mid-1950s.

One quiet Saturday night I walked over to the Tabernacle. It was open, so I went in. Nobody was there but me. Broken, I just put my face in the rug; I was crying out to God. Eventually, I rose and paced over to the platform to where the organ was, praying aloud, "Lord, if I could only play the organ… if I could just play the organ for You…"

Just then, the Lord clearly replied: *I didn't call you to play the organ. I have called you to play on the heart strings of men with the Word of God.* I never again, after that, asked God to let me play a musical instrument. He made it clear what my calling was.

As my dear friends and I prayed for direction, I began to consider quitting my job and going into full-time ministry. During this time, I received a call from a leading full gospel group based on the West Coast who was looking for a worship leader for one of their traveling teams. At first, it seemed like a confirmation.

This group had conferences in some of the nation's largest venues, like Madison Square Garden and San Francisco's Cow Palace. I promised to pray about the offer.

I knew it was next to impossible to break into ministry as a single woman unless you were a soloist or a musician. Since I didn't have those talents, I thought I might be able to become a singer like Cliff Barrows, who led the music for Billy Graham.

"This might be the biggest chance I'll ever get," I mused.

I had nearly convinced myself I should take this offer when, as I was driving to work one morning along Shore Drive in Corpus, I heard the Lord speaking to me. *You didn't ask Me,* said the still small Voice.

"Of course," I responded, "but this offer *has* to be from You."

His answer was firm, *Better that you should preach to a few than sing for the thousands.*

The words took the wind right out of my sails, and I turned the offer down. I would continue to wait upon whatever God had for me—in ministry as well as marriage.

Chapter 4
Surrender

Evangelist Anne Nethery
promotional photo

Born to Preach

Chapter 4
Surrender

"Commit your way to the LORD, trust also in Him, and He shall bring it to pass."

—Psalm 37:5 (NKJV)

During the time that I led the worship services at church, a couple from California—Beauford and Sally Dowel—visited the Tabernacle. They came for several services and afterwards asked me to join their traveling evangelistic team as a worship leader.

I felt the time had come to step into ministry, so, impulsively, I quit my job and made the trip to Dallas, expecting to join the Dowels for services at a church founded by the well-known healing evangelist, Jack Coe.

When I arrived, however, there was a problem. The Dowels didn't need a worship leader for those specific services. Seeing my disappointment, they quickly offered me an alternative. I could go to Ft. Worth, where their friends, the Sherwoods, pastored a small storefront church. They assured me this couple would be open for me to hold meetings there.

Born to Preach

I agreed to go, and leaving my car at my Aunt Ruby's house, the Dowels put me on a bus for Ft. Worth. I preached in their church every night for a week, and God blessed. They asked me to stay and preach another week, and I accepted, but insisted on having Monday off. I hadn't heard anything from the Dowels, and I needed to get back to Dallas and find out what their plans were, and whether or not those plans still included me.

The Sherwoods were so kind and helpful and loaned me their extra vehicle—a heavy duty truck—so I could drive over to the trailer park where the Dowels had been staying. Upon arriving, I learned to my great amazement that they had left two days earlier for meetings in California, without saying a word to me.

That night, I stayed at my Aunt Myrtle's house and the next day drove back to Ft. Worth to complete my week of preaching. Actually, I didn't know anything else to do. I no longer had a job to go back to. I was truly alone and "on my own."

My routine each day was to get up, have breakfast, and spend the morning in prayer and Bible study. In the afternoon, I would hike along the highway to a small grocery store and purchase two Snickers bars for a snack; one I ate on the way back to the Sherwoods and the other I ate after church.

One day as I was walking along, kicking gravel and talking to the Lord about my dire situation, I heard Him speaking to my heart.

Daughter, if you will obey Me, you will never need a man to put a roof over your head, food in your mouth or shoes on your feet. I will take care of you. You just obey Me and do what I've called you to do.

Chapter 4: Surrender

The words would prove prophetic not only in the next few weeks but in all the years that followed.

∽৶৽

When my second week of preaching ended, I decided to go to Beaumont from Dallas. My friend Bobbie and her husband, Rod, had recently moved there from Corpus Christi. Once again, I rented a room in their home. For several months, Bobbie and I held services in a number of small churches in the area, until the Lord began dealing with me about returning to Corpus Christi.

"Oh, God, I *can't* go back home," I protested. I had only been gone for about eighteen months, and I was enjoying my work and being on my own.

One day, I wrestled with the Lord all day long over the prospect of returning to Corpus Christi. By now, I had retrieved my car from my aunt's house in Dallas where it had been parked. I *could* drive home, but Corpus was 300 miles from Beaumont. "I've never driven that far alone before," I objected.

Are you going to stay here because you've never driven that distance before? He asked. *Or, are you going to go because I told you to?*

At the end of the day, I told the Lord I would obey Him.

The next day, I again debated the idea of leaving for Corpus, telling the Lord I didn't have any money. (Actually, I had about eight dollars—barely enough for gas.) Well-meaning friends encouraged me to stay put and not return home; but their advice only made my decision more difficult.

Born to Preach

I had no peace. All day long, the Lord probed my thoughts with questions. *Are you going to stay here because you don't have the money? Or, will you go because I told you?*

By the third day, I was physically sick, with my knees buckling at the prospect of going back. Yet again, the Lord presented me with a question. *Are you going to stay here because you're sick, or are you going because I told you to go?*

Finally, I surrendered. I felt so strongly and clearly about returning home, and in obedience, I went. At six o'clock the next morning, I got into my car and drove off in a pouring rain. Fortunately, gasoline was about nineteen cents a gallon at the time, and I arrived in Corpus with only change in my purse.

Mother answered my knock on the front door. Since leaving home, I had lost several pounds from the anxiety of being out on my own without any dependable income. Mother's face registered her surprise at seeing her much-thinner daughter standing before her. She recovered quickly, however and invited me in.

I got right to the point. "The Lord has told me to come back to Corpus," I explained. "Would you mind if I stayed a few days?"

"That would be *fine*," she said, smiling warmly. Both she and my father were surprisingly cordial about my return and seemed genuinely happy to have me home.

When I came back home, I was decidedly broke, so when my pastor asked me to speak at the Wednesday night service, I was pleased. *Surely*, I thought, *He will bless me with an offering.*

But I was wrong. The service ended, and I got into my car to drive home with my wallet still sadly empty—but not for long.

Chapter 4: Surrender

The next morning, my mother handed me fifteen dollars. "Your daddy wants you to have this," she said casually.

"But why?" I asked. "Where'd this come from?"

"He sold some paint a few weeks back and they brought him the money yesterday," she explained. "He went out to the car to leave for work this morning, came back and said, 'Give this to Anne. She needs it more than I do.'"

What a surprise! My father would have been the last person I would have expected to give me money. God's hand was continually being shown in sending me back home.

I also saw a change in my relationship with my mother. We began praying together for a specific job for me. "God, if there's not a job, please create one," we prayed.

Mother told me that's what she had prayed during the Depression when my father was out of work and had knocked on doors for weeks with no results. The very day she prayed that prayer, he had gone to a radio station—where he'd been many times before—and applied for a position.

That day, an announcer hadn't shown up for work, and Daddy was given the job—one for which he had no training or experience. It was truly a gift from the Lord.

God also answered my mother's prayer for a job for me. I soon found a good position with Atlantic Refining Company, at *double* the pay I had made before. Three months later, the company moved its entire oil and gas accounting office down to Corpus from Dallas. Eventually, I became head of my department.

I began attending services again at the Tabernacle and soon found myself back in the position of the church worship leader.

But I was decidedly unhappy. I felt restless, and wished I could begin my ministry in earnest, getting right to the heart of my calling. Yet, I knew that God had His own timetable, and I would simply have to wait.

At first, I thought returning to Corpus was for the sake of my family. Then, one day, right after coming back, the Lord spoke to me, saying, *I have something to teach you.*

I thought, "This won't take long; I'm teachable."

Just as surely as I told you when you should come back here, the Lord instructed, *I will tell you when to leave.*

❧

My best friend at the time was JoEllen Forbus, and I often confided in her. A pretty blonde, she was a talented musician and singer and served as the church organist. One day, as I was driving her home after church, I complained about my situation.

"I know God has brought me back here, but I can hardly stand it sometimes," I said. "I'm just about to come out of my skin. I know being here is God's will for me, but I want to be out doing ministry."

As I drove off from JoEllen's house, the Lord spoke to me. *Daughter, bitter and sweet water cannot come out of the same fountain. You're saying you know it's God from one side of your mouth but the other side is saying you can hardly stand it.*

I was devastated by God's words to me, and sorrow filled my heart. Tears streamed down my face as I drove. "Lord, what do You want me to say?" I asked.

Chapter 4: Surrender

You say what David said, 'I delight to do Thy will, oh my God.' That's when I learned never to qualify what that will has to be— just as long as it was God's will."

Through clinched teeth I began to confess, "I delight to do Thy will, oh God," even though I didn't fully mean it. The second day, I continued, and it got a little easier. By the third day, I could say it much more freely, and began to mean it.

I learned God's will isn't necessarily a bed of roses or even something you might like. It might feel constraining. Nonetheless, it contains a grace that enables one to accomplish His purpose in the face of every challenge.

During this time, I received occasional invitations to minister. One day, I was on an airplane flying to Houston to preach when the Lord spoke to me about my family. *You think you have to be in Corpus for your family because everyone depends on you,* He said. *But if you'll obey My calling upon your life, I'll save every one of them…and if you don't, you'll be in the way and I'll have to deal with you.*

That was a strong word, but I believed it was true…and I chose to obey.

It wasn't long before I saw the results of that commitment. One day when I came home from work, my mother met me at the front door. "Come in and *hurry*," she said, worry evident in her voice, "and pray for your daddy."

He was in a back bedroom on the bed shaking and crying, his face and clothes soaked in perspiration. "Pray for him," Mother urged.

I shook my head "no." "He doesn't want me to do that," I responded, acutely aware of how resistant to God my father had always been. "He doesn't want me to touch him."

"He wants you to pray for him," she insisted, giving me a pleading look.

I relented, stepped over to his bedside, intending to pray a nice, quiet prayer. Instead, when I placed my hand on his back and opened my mouth, I roared like a lion. Fervent prayer came pouring out of my mouth. I started speaking in tongues and just kept praying and praying—not quietly, but at the top of my lungs.

After several minutes, I sensed he was calming down, and soon, he stopped shaking and crying. Finally, I stopped praying in tongues and hurried out of the bedroom, trying to grasp what had just happened.

I didn't understand until several weeks later that Daddy was having a nervous breakdown. He was forced to take a leave of absence from work and spend most of his days at home on the living room couch.

Thereafter, this scenario became an everyday occurrence for the next six weeks or so. I would pray for my father each day when I came home, and he would always get better. I found that he knew absolutely nothing about God—not even about Christmas or Easter. I would sit there and tell him Bible stories, describing, as one would to a child, the accounts of Abraham, Jonathan, and Joshua—he knew nothing of them.

One day my mother asked me to go in and pray for him, and I said, "*Mother*! There is nothing else left to pray for him unless I say, 'Hail Mary, Mother of grace'…there is just nothing left!"

Chapter 4: Surrender

She said, "I don't care what you pray, just go in there and pray for him."

Then, one Sunday night, the Lord told me to stay home from church. Daddy was lying on the couch reading a book and Mother was sitting in a chair by the front door doing needlework.

Finally I spoke up. "Daddy," I began, "I've carried you as far as I can on my faith. I believe God will completely heal you if you'll accept Him as your Lord and Savior. He's done a lot already, but I believe He'll finish it if you'll just receive Him."

With that, I got out of my chair, knelt down and started praying. I didn't have any idea what my father would say or do. At one point, I glanced over my shoulder and saw my mother kneeling beside her chair. Shortly afterwards, Daddy was on his knees in front of the couch, giving his heart to the Lord.

Miracle of miracles! I had never before seen my parents on their knees praying to God.

Later that night, Daddy called my sister to tell her the good news. "All this time I thought she'd thrown her life away," he told Beverly, "but today I found out that she's the only one who was really living!"

It was several weeks before Daddy returned to his job as a television news commentator. Then, his doctor inexplicably prescribed shock treatments for his condition.

I objected strenuously. "Heavens no!" I told my mother. "He's gotten saved and shock treatments will leave him unable to remember a thing."

"But that's what the doctor's recommending," she countered.

In the midst of talking over the shock treatments, the Lord spoke to me. *It's with the heart that man believes unto righteousness and the mouth confesses salvation...It's not the mind.*

God gave me His word on the matter, and that settled the issue for me. I knew that Daddy would recover in spite of the treatments.

Amazingly, my father had the first treatment and came out praising God and witnessing to everybody at the hospital. He reacted in the same way after the second treatment, even telling his boss about the great things God had done.

During this time, my friends Bobbie and Rod Newland had again moved, this time from Beaumont to Shreveport, Louisiana, but they often came to Corpus for conventions at the Tabernacle. They were now in town for a conference featuring David Schoch, a prophet from California. I prepared to go back to Shreveport with them for a week's vacation.

Recently, Bobbie and I had been making plans for once again doing ministry together. Her husband, we figured, could continue with his job in Shreveport while we ministered in church services and spoke at conferences. But it was not to be.

Bobbie and I intended to leave for Shreveport before the conference ended. The night before we were to leave, however, I sensed I wasn't to make the trip. Instead, I decided to stay in Corpus for the last few days of the convention. It would prove to be a life-and-death decision.

Chapter 4: Surrender

Early the next morning, Bobbie and another friend, Elma Simmons, left for Louisiana. Shortly afterwards, they were involved in a grinding head-on collision between Beaumont and Houston. Bobbie was killed instantly. Elma was thrown from the car and suffered major injuries that left her terribly disfigured.

With Bobbie gone, it seemed my dreams of full-time ministry would remain just that—dreams. I felt more alone than ever. I was twenty-six and still single, still leading the worship service at church, and still living at home with my parents.

In the aftermath of Bobbie's sudden passing, the future looked dark and uninviting. Then, one night as I was praying in my bedroom, I heard these words: *Come on through the knot hole, Baby.*

The voice reminded me of Bobbie's. She had given me the nickname "Baby" because I was younger. Those words gave me the comfort and encouragement that I sorely needed.

As difficult as it was, I knew I would get through this loss of such a close friend. Perhaps I had placed too much emphasis on working together with Bobbie in ministry. I was devastated with her gone; I needed to refocus my life and ministry. If I continued to obey God, He would bring to pass His plans for me, just as He had promised.

Obviously, I was to move forward in my calling, but just where, I had no idea. Surely, I told myself, the Lord will give me His fresh direction.

Born to Preach

Chapter 5
Learning to Trust God

Anne preaching in Detroit 1965

Born to Preach

Chapter 5

Learning to Trust God

"I've come to realize that the greatest gift anyone can have is the capacity to hear God's voice. Because 'faith comes by hearing', it is essential. If I can simply hear His voice, there is no problem in life I cannot face."

—Anne Gimenez

As I awaited the Lord's direction, I couldn't help but notice the change of scenery around me. Some of the young people in the church began to marry and have children, and a few went into the ministry. I was seemingly left behind, with no immediate prospect of doing either.

One Sunday morning as I was leaving church, I encountered an elderly man with a cane, making his way toward the back door. "When are *you* going out in the ministry?" he asked abruptly.

I was taken aback by his question. "Whenever the Lord tells me," I answered, somewhat lamely.

He shook his head. "Well, it looks like to me He told you a long time ago," he said pointedly.

Born to Preach

His words struck like a dagger in my heart, and my eyes began to burn with tears. I wanted nothing more than to go into ministry. On the way home I told the Lord, "If I was a man, I would have already gone into ministry a long time ago."

I had been raised under a pastoral team who taught that, if you were called to ministry, you ought to drive down the street to the first church, knock on the door, and ask to preach. My pastor saw the church as a "sending station" for the called ones—not a rest stop for the saints.

The pressure to find my place in ministry was as ever-present as the expectation for me to settle down. Over the years, I had received several marriage proposals, including one from my high school beau, Waymond. He had asked, "Would you marry me like I am?"

I loved him very much, but in my heart I knew I could never marry someone who wouldn't serve God or wasn't going into ministry. That would have never worked for me. When my relationship with that young man eventually ended, I decided I would probably never marry.

❧❧

I found myself fresh out of high school and with Waymond out of the picture, newly single. I knew beyond the shadow of a doubt that I was called to preach, but I didn't have the slightest idea of where to start. I was so positive that I was going into the ministry that I prepared for it.

If I bought a dress, I would look at it through the lenses of, "Is this something that I could preach in?" Everything I bought was for travel. It was always a suitcase, a travel iron, or a travel alarm clock. In everything that I did, I was preparing for my calling. Now it seemed that I would be serving Jesus as a single.

In addition to breaking up with Waymond, I faced other character-building situations during this time. Eventually, I would see that these experiences helped prepare me to be genuinely used of God.

For example, one day while talking with my mother in my bedroom, I decided to probe her thoughts about my plans. "Mother, do you believe I'm called to preach?" I asked.

She thought for a moment. "Well," she replied slowly, "now that you mention it, I've never really been quite sure." And she walked out of the room without another word.

I thought, *I'm going to have a nervous breakdown right now. I've earned it and I deserve it. If my own mother doesn't believe in me, what hope do I have?*

"Lord, why did she say that to me?" I questioned.

The answer came immediately.

If you have to ask any man about your calling, you're not called, He spoke to my heart. *Don't ever ask anyone again whether or not you're called. That's between Me and you.*

❧ ❧

When I started out in the ministry, all I had was a King James Bible, a Cruden's Concordance, and a Webster's Dictionary. That's all. I never had the opportunity to go to Bible School; I served in my church, and that was my Bible School. I did everything: preached wherever, talked with whomever, spoke on the radio—did everything that they asked me to do.

I never went through formal ministry training, so I only knew one way to prepare a sermon. The only way I knew to get a message was to get on my knees and pray until I heard a word in my spirit. Then, I would get up and research that word, and that's what I would preach.

Somebody once asked me, "When you travel, what do you preach about? Do you have a portfolio?" I responded that I have never had a portfolio, and, to my knowledge, I've never preached the same message twice! Nobody ever told me you could preach the same message twice! I had a new one every time. Every, single time I preached, I would get on my knees.

Sometimes, I would preach every morning and evening, and I often spent my waking hours on my knees. I would pray until I got a word from God—for example, "grace." Then, I would study that word using my Cruden's Concordance—there was no computer to pull it up on the screen. I wrote all my messages out by hand; I made all my notes by hand. That's the only way I knew to preach.

❧

In spite of those who, like my mother, doubted my calling, churches began inviting me as their Sunday speaker, and I preached frequent revivals in several small towns nearby. But since I was the main worship leader at the Tabernacle, I needed to be present for most of the services there.

Then, one day Pastor Salstrand called asking if I would preach a series of revival meetings in my home church. I was thrilled. He said we'd begin about three weeks away on a Sunday. I immediately threw myself into preparation for the services, and gave no thought to the fact that he made no further mention of the meetings.

The revival was to begin on a Sunday night. That morning, Brother Salstrand approached me right before the service. "Do you *really* want to preach this week?" he asked.

I looked at him, sensing that something had changed in our original plans. "Well, that's up to you," I responded.

"Well, if you really don't want to preach this week, Sidney and Lavonne just came in last night," he explained, "and they don't have any meetings…so, if you don't really want to preach, we'll just let Sidney preach."

Lavonne was his daughter, and his son-in-law, Sidney, had just become an evangelist. I felt tears welling up, but I didn't want to cry in front of him. "Is that all right?" he asked again.

"You're the pastor," I replied, carefully controlling my voice.

So, I went out to the platform and led the worship service. Afterwards, I sat down on the front row as Brother Salstrand walked to the pulpit. "Sister Anne was going to preach this week," he began. "I don't know what happened but I guess she didn't have enough messages or something, so Sidney and Lavonne are going to preach."

I wished that I was invisible as the pastor laughed and teased about the services, and tears streamed quietly down my cheeks. I was glad I had taken a seat on the front row; hopefully, no one could see my face.

"Oh, God," I prayed in silent desperation, "Please say something to me." When I reached down and opened my Bible, my eyes immediately focused upon the words of 1 Peter 5:6, "Humble yourselves therefore under the mighty hand of God, that He may exalt you in due time" (NKJV).

As I savored the words of Scripture, I heard God's voice speaking in my innermost being. *Daughter, this is not your time, but when your time comes, you will not need a man to exalt you. I will lift you up.*

I felt comforted that God's plan for my life was still at work, even though I had been shuffled aside and not permitted to preach that night. But I still wanted to stay home instead of leading the music for somebody else's revival.

Oh, you're going to come and lead the worship services, the Lord confirmed to me. *You're going to speak in tongues, shout, and prophesy.*

And I did. It was a great character-building time in my life, and before long, God released me into full time ministry.

❧❧

March of 1963 was a month like no other—a pivotal time in my life. Brother Harry Hodge, who had shaped and influenced countless lives since the 1920s—including mine—was called to heaven.

It was that very same month I *knew* the time had finally come to step into full-time ministry, and I gave three weeks notice at my job. I didn't tell my pastor ahead of time that I intended to leave. For one thing, I knew he was not fully supportive of my desire to preach.

Chapter 5: Learning to Trust God

He had once told my best friend, JoEllen, that I'd never succeed in full-time ministry. "There are a lot of men who are better preachers than her," he had observed, "and they can't make it. Why would we think she could?" Besides, I didn't want to take a chance that he might announce my plans prematurely.

One Sunday shortly before I quit my job, I sat in the sanctuary with my friends as the pastor taught the Sunday School lesson. When he finished, he abruptly asked the class, "How many of you know that Sister Anne is leaving?"

Everybody looked at him—stunned. I could hardly believe my ears. "How could he possibly have found out?" I asked myself.

Pleased with his audience's reaction, Brother Salstrand went on. "Yes, she's getting married," he teased. It was an odd quirk in his personality, but he often found things funny that no one else did.

JoEllen's husband, Bobby, nudged me. "We'll leave if you want to go," he offered. I declined, knowing the Lord had already told me to lead the worship service as usual. Although the pastor had humiliated me, mocking the fact that I was unmarried, I resolved that I would not walk out.

As the pastor concluded, I stepped up to the platform. "I was driving down Shore Drive on my way home from work the other day," I began, "telling the Lord I would have already gone into ministry if I had been a man."

People stirred and sat up as I spoke.

"The Lord told me," I continued, "that He'd given me everything I needed for the ministry in gifts except the grace to go. But

He told me when the day comes, I would have the grace…and I just want you to know that today I have the grace to go."

The next Wednesday evening, I preached at my home church. When I finished, the pastor prepared to close the service. Evidently, he hadn't planned to receive a collection for me. Then, someone in the back interrupted.

"We always take an offering for speakers here," the man suggested, "especially our own." With that, people from every corner of the building started bringing an offering to the altar.

❧

The following week I preached in Channelview, Texas—the town where Aunt Ruby and the little Assembly of God church had touched my heart as a child—every morning and night for thirteen services.

On the last night of meetings, my sister called from Corpus Christi about midnight to say her husband had been filled with the Holy Spirit. Dick had been led to the Lord years before under Lester Roloff's ministry at the Alameda Street Baptist Church.

Afterwards, however, he had sensed that something still seemed to be missing from his life, and he undertook a long search. In the process, he discovered that the gifts of the Holy Spirit had not disappeared when the last Apostle left the earth. They were still available to every believer. Dick opened his heart to receive everything the Lord had for him.

Beverly put Dick on the phone. "What happened to you?" I asked happily.

Chapter 5: Learning to Trust God

"I don't know," he laughed. "But I do know it started at my feet and came out my mouth…I'll never be the same again."

I went back to my room thinking, *Lord, this is too wonderful for me.* It touched me deeply to see the hand of God on my family.

Lying on the bed in the darkness, I heard Him speaking to me. *That's the beginning. I told you I would deliver and fill every one of them.*

From that meeting in Channelview, I went on to a church in Houston for what was planned as a week-long series. But as the first week of services concluded, the crowds were still spirited. "Let's go another week," the pastor suggested.

He had received love offerings several times during that first week. "Since we're going another week, I'll give you a check at the end of next week," the pastor promised.

I preached another week with good results and fresh anointing in the services. As promised, the pastor gave me a check the last night. I had been staying at his home, so the next morning I packed my bags and left about nine o'clock. Curiously, neither the pastor nor his wife got up to say goodbye.

I stopped for gas before getting out of town on my trip to Victoria, Texas, and looked at the check. It was for two hundred dollars. My heart sank.

This has to be a mistake, I thought to myself. Attendance at the meetings had been excellent, and it was highly likely that the pastor had received over two hundred dollars the *first* week.

Then it dawned on me. "Could it really be that he kept back some of the offering?" I wondered to myself. Tears filled my eyes.

I could not help but wonder, "Would he have treated me so brazenly if I had been a man?"

"Lord, please say something to me," I said, reaching over for my Bible. I looked down as the pages opened, and my eyes fastened on the words of Psalm 105:15, "...Touch not mine anointed, and do my prophets no harm" (KJV).

Daughter, I will take care of you, I felt the Lord speaking to me, *and I will take care of him.*

I never looked back and I never heard from that pastor and his wife in Houston again. God blessed the meetings the next week in Victoria, and afterwards, I was on my way to Ft. Worth to preach my next meeting.

I don't know when I learned to hear God's voice in the midst of a crisis, but the gift became a vital part of my life. I learned if God spoke to me about any issue—and if I knew it was God's voice—I could rely solely on whatever He said. I could face any challenge and still go forward. This truth became a cornerstone of my life.

❧

After those meetings, I went several weeks without receiving any invitations at all. One day, I called Brother Salstrand to see if he knew of any churches where I might preach. But when I hung up the phone, I felt burdened and got down on my knees to pray.

The Lord spoke to me: *If you are going to depend on the arm of flesh, you'd better call and see if you can get your old job back... you're going to need it. But, if you depend on Me, you will never need a man to open a door for you.*

Chapter 5: Learning to Trust God

I quickly repented. The next day, when Brother Salstrand called back saying he could get no meetings for me, I felt greatly relieved and rejoiced in my spirit. I knew God would open the right doors, and I never again lacked invitations to preach.

One Sunday, I was on my way to preach in a little church in Ingleside. It was pouring rain that day, but the Lord impressed me to stop at my sister's house and pray for their family. They now had four children and were facing some difficult financial problems.

As I prayed over Beverly that day, the Lord spoke to me saying He was going to supply their need through "an unexpected source." We praised the Lord together and I promised to stay in touch.

It was still raining the next morning when I left Ingleside for Houston. As I drove, I heard the Lord say, *Send your sister $100.* A hundred dollars was nearly all I had left in the bank to cover my car payment, and the $20 offering I had just received was my travel money. But I dutifully pulled off at a gas station, got a cup of coffee, and addressed a letter to Beverly with the check.

As I wrote the note, I heard the Lord whisper to my heart, *Tell her that she doesn't have to pay it back!*

The "unexpected source" turned out to be me. That seed offering was a test of my obedience, and became a turning point opening unexpected doors. I kept learning that obedience to God is a mighty spiritual weapon.

A few days later, I was in Louisiana, sitting in an arbor meeting with my friend, Ruth Forbus, when the preacher pointed to me and said, "You have the call of God upon your life. Doors will surely open for you, daughter."

Born to Preach

❧

At that same brush arbor meeting, I met a woman known simply as "Sister Carter." She pastored a small congregation in the town of Waller, which was about forty miles northwest of Houston. She invited me to preach for a week.

Waller had about 700 people at the time and was so small that when you passed under the blinking light in the center of town, you were on your way out the other side.

I stopped at a church where I thought I was supposed to be that morning and sat down in the back. Sunday School was underway, but Sister Carter was nowhere to be seen. Perplexed, I finally asked someone where she was. As it turned out, I was in the wrong church.

Sister Carter's church was a few blocks over. When I finally walked in, the praise and worship was just concluding. "Sister Anne Nethery is here now," the pastor announced. "We're going to bring her up to preach right now."

Usually, I liked to feel the spirit of a church before leading a service but there was no chance to do so that morning. So, I walked to the platform and preached.

Sister Carter was a large, buxom woman with blonde hair pulled straight back in a bun. After the service, she came up to me and announced, "I don't have any place for you to sleep here, but let me see if you can stay at the lady's house that plays the organ." I groaned a little inwardly, realizing she had made no preparation for me. I had no idea of the comical and bewildering scenario that was about to unfold.

Chapter 5: Learning to Trust God

The organist was in her mid-sixties and her salt-and-pepper hair was cut in a Dutch boy style that reminded me of one of the Three Stooges. Arrangements were made for me to stay with her, and I followed her out a winding road into the countryside to a drab old wooden house with floor-to-ceiling windows.

We stood on the front porch and chatted a few minutes before going inside. Suddenly, she remarked, "I used to have a little dog and and he barked a lot, but he doesn't bark anymore."

It was an odd remark, inserted abruptly into the conversation, and I wondered to myself, "Why doesn't the dog bark anymore?"

That night, we went back to church and I preached both Sunday and Monday nights. One of those nights, the pastor's father was there. "I'm sure glad to see you," he said, as if he hadn't expected to. "I've looked for you every night...boy, the devil would sure like to kill him a preacher!"

His strange comment puzzled me, but I didn't dwell on it. Unfortunately, his meaning became clear soon enough.

For some reason, I sensed that it would not be wise to eat anything that I didn't see my hostess eat while I was there. One day, I had to go into the kitchen while she was out of the house, and I noticed long butcher knives in virtually every drawer. Then, walking past her bedroom, I saw a long butcher knife on the table beside her bed.

"What kind of place am I in?" I wondered to myself. I was beginning to fell uneasy about my situation.

The shotgun-style house had rooms on either side of a long hallway, and the woman had given me the front bedroom.

Tuesday night, I was asleep in the darkened room, lying on my left side, when I saw (as in a vision) my hostess standing over my bed with a butcher knife in her hand, poised to strike.

"Oh, my God," I mumbled, and began praying in tongues and rebuking the devil. "*What* am I seeing?"

When I opened my eyes, I saw what appeared to be a large snake with the woman's face as its head. By now, I had rolled over into the middle of the bed and was praying even harder. Then I looked over at the door and saw two shadowy figures that I believed were angels on either side of the door frame.

She won't come through that door tonight, the Lord assured me.

"God, when I see daylight I'm getting out of here," I said. But the next day, Wednesday, I started talking myself out of moving. "I'm just tired and nervous," I told myself.

On Wednesday night, Joy Heath, a friend from Houston, came for the evening service. When she asked where I was staying, I said "With the organist."

"You are *not!*" she exclaimed, as if unsure she had heard me correctly.

"Yeah, I really am."

"Well, I'll drive you back and forth every night myself," she promised. "I've heard everybody in this town talking about how that woman tried to murder her husband."

Joy took swift action and confronted Sister Carter, demanding that she immediately move me out of the organist's house to another location. Sister Carter eventually agreed that I could room with her daughter until we closed the revival meetings.

Chapter 5: Learning to Trust God

When Sister Carter's daughter and I went back out to get my suitcases, the organist's menacing attitude confirmed my suspicions. She was decidedly hostile, mumbling under her breath and glaring at me. Later, I heard that her deceased husband had told people she'd stood over his bed with a knife in hand. And he had died in the *very* bed I had been using.

Sharing a bedroom at Sister Carter's had its own hazards. Her daughter was a cat lover, and I wound up with a bad case of ringworms. To get rid of them, Mother ultimately had to put my clothes in the bathtub and soak them in kerosene. Strange and humorous occurrences like these were sometimes commonplace on the evangelistic field and this was only my first year out in full-time evangelism.

One day while I was still in Waller, Sister Carter suggested we attend a morning service at the Stude Revival Center in Houston, pastored by Fred Marcum. When she introduced me as the evangelist speaking at her church, Pastor Marcum asked, "Do you have a word for us?"

I had already prepared my message for that night in Waller, so I replied, "Yes, I do." So, I preached that morning in one of the biggest churches I'd ever spoken in. Afterwards, the pastor asked if I would come and preach an entire week at the Center. I gladly agreed.

❧❧

About a week later, I drove to Houston to attend the morning service at the Center. Some 600 people were packed into the pews. The size of the crowd scared the living daylights out of me.

I was used to preaching to churches of twenty or thirty—or less. Now, I was about to preach to hundreds.

That afternoon, I went to God in prayer. "I want to go home," I lamented. "I'm scared and I want to go home."

The Lord began speaking to me. *I want you to do what David did.*

"What did he do, Lord?" I asked.

He used what he had.

"God, these people have had the biggest and best come to this church," I suggested.

Just use what you have, He said.

What I had was simply a word I had received during my time of study and prayer with the Lord. That was the key—receiving a fresh and distinctive word from heaven. Then, I could genuinely declare that "this word" is what God is saying *today* to His people.

I preached that night and each night for the rest of the week, and taught over the church's daily radio program. The pastor was pleased with the results. "I want you to stay another week," he enthused.

The second week, Pastor Marcum asked if I had ever heard of Pastor Allie Taylor from Detroit. I didn't know her, but he said she'd called his office the day before asking about me.

"She'd received our church flyer announcing Anne Nethery was preaching here for a second week," he continued. "She said any woman who can preach for a man and hold people's interest for two weeks can *really* preach. She's going to be calling you."

Chapter 5: Learning to Trust God

Sure enough, Pastor Taylor called, and I was soon on an airplane flying to Detroit. God blessed the meetings at Lighthouse Tabernacle; they ran a week, and then she, too, asked me to stay over another week.

Pastor Taylor asked one day if I knew about the Revival Center in Pittsburgh. "Not at all," I answered.

"Well, they'd like you," she promised, "and I'm going to call them."

So, during that same trip north, I preached in Pittsburgh's Revival Center, as well as several smaller churches in that Pennsylvania valley. In one of them, I met Bea Lamont, a friendly, colorful woman preacher who would become a life-long friend.

She also would one day introduce me to a person who would change my life forever.

Born to Preach

Chapter 6
A Leap of Faith

Preaching in McKeysport, Pennsylvania
for Bea Lamont 1965

Born to Preach

Chapter 6

A Leap of Faith

"So also faith, if it does not have works (deeds and actions of obedience to back it up), by itself is destitute of power (inoperative, dead)."

—*James 2:17 (Amplified Bible)*

Even though I kept busy traveling and holding meetings, I struggled with loneliness. No friends or people from my former church encouraged or supported me as I ventured forth, and my parents were totally against what I was doing. Frequently, when I left Corpus Christi to hold meetings in other locations, I cried my way down the road.

In the midst of one late night drive, the Lord spoke to me: *When are you going to leave your funeral?*

Suddenly, I pictured myself standing looking down at a casket, and I knew what He was telling me. I was weeping over the death of my flesh, my self-life. I was grieved and hurt over my church's ignoring my years of service and my family's open hostility to my calling, and my emotional upheaval was hindering me from ministering as effectively as I could.

God's question ended my weeping. I got the point; I understood it was my funeral.

Shortly after this experience, the postman brought me a letter containing an invitation from a church in Chicago. Now, being from south Texas, Chicago was the "big time" for me. "Am I really ready for this?" I wondered.

That afternoon, I had to leave for Louisiana, and I decided to stop off in Baytown, Texas, to see an old friend, Ruth Forbus, and get her thoughts about this special invitation.

Ruth didn't mince words. "Oh, no," she said, her brow furrowing. "You shouldn't do that. You shouldn't be traveling to a place like that."

"Why not?" I inquired.

"That's not a safe place," she continued. "My husband would never let me drive that distance all alone."

Ruth's reaction surprised me. She had been a strong woman of faith for many years and had a genuine prophetic gift. "Lord, why is she trying to discourage me?" I asked, as I drove away from her house. Would I, a woman alone, be doing a foolish thing, heading into the Big City by myself?

I didn't tell <u>her</u> to go to Chicago, He replied. *I told <u>you</u>. She doesn't have the faith for it.*

Without further delay, I accepted the invitation and headed north. It was December 1963. While still many miles south of Chicago, I encountered my first snowstorm and began looking for a place to stop for the night. When at last I spotted what was once called a "tourist camp"—a series of small wooden cabins built around a semi-circular driveway—I pulled in.

Chapter 6: A Leap of Faith

The motel's caretaker, an elderly man wrapped in a heavy coat, took a handful of keys, led me to one of the cabins, opened the door for me, and turned the heat on in the room. I felt very vulnerable, and as soon as the door closed behind him, I placed a chair in front of it. Then, with the blizzard swirling outside, I got under all the blankets and I began to pray.

"Lord, there's not a soul in this world who knows me who knows where I am tonight or even cares," I prayed. Feeling quite forlorn, I thought about my family. They never called or contacted me unless there was some emergency. Tonight, they couldn't even do that. God truly had to be my keeper.

The next day was clear, and I continued on. At last, after two full days of driving, I arrived in downtown Chicago and learned I was to preach in a former nightclub down in the Bowery district. The premises, I was told, had been recently renovated and were now being used for church services. To my surprise, I also learned the pastor was out of town and wouldn't be attending any of the meetings.

He had left instructions for me, however, and I followed them carefully for the entire week, conducting the services, receiving the offerings, and giving the altar calls.

Early in the week, several church members told me that visiting evangelists often had their cars stolen while doing services there. I was staying in a rundown hotel near the church and had parked my new Chevrolet right outside where I could keep an eye on it. That same night, I went outside and prayed over it. At the end of the week, my Chevy was still in its place, untouched and unharmed. And so was I.

Born to Preach

Looking back on my introduction to the "Windy City", I was thankful I had listened to God and not given into fears for my safety. I never again hesitated to accept an invitation to preach in a big city—or any other possibly unsafe location.

$\approx$

In early January 1964, I was back in Texas, holding services in Victoria. One day before dawn, I was walking around in the church's sanctuary praying, when the Lord spoke to me. *Before the month is over, your feet will be on foreign soil.*

For several days, I wondered what God had in store. Then one morning, I received a call from Pastors Herbert and Rita Sweat, at whose church in Little Washington, Pennsylvania, I had once preached. They wanted to know if I would accompany them on a trip to Jamaica at the end of January.

Their phone call was my needed confirmation. Within two weeks, the Sweats and I, along with Jonathan and Barbara Gulla, who were musicians, were standing on Jamaican soil, holding outdoor meetings with both preaching and music, first in Montego Bay and then in Kingston.

Another group was holding a church convention in the same area, and they kindly invited us to participate in their meetings. When Herb volunteered me to preach, the convention leaders declined. "No," they replied emphatically. "We don't have women preaching in our meetings."

Herb did not argue. He replied simply, "Each of our team members will get up and greet the people." When it came my turn to speak, I had already learned, especially as a woman, not to take advantage of such an opportunity. I would do what I was asked and not overstep my boundaries.

Each of us had five minutes to share. I spoke briefly out of Isaiah and sat down; as I did, the people jumped to their feet and shouted.

Afterwards, I saw the convention's leader walk down to Herb. "He wants to know if you'll preach tomorrow night, the last night of their meeting," Herb told me. I accepted the invitation, and, as it turned out, it was the largest night meeting of their entire convention. When it was over, I was asked to stay an additional three days and preach in their church, which I gladly did.

Our hosts then drove me back to Montego Bay where I rejoined "the team" for additional street meetings. We planned to fly to Haiti two days later and hold meetings there before we returned to the states.

The day after I arrived in Montego Bay, however, I suddenly began to feel an urge to take an early flight back to Corpus Christi. At first, it was an uneasy feeling in my spirit, but the more I prayed, the more it intensified. I wrestled with that conviction throughout the day and finally spoke to Herb.

"Are you sure?" he asked.

I nodded my head. "I don't understand it but I believe it's God," I answered.

"Well, if you're going, you'll need to go today because if you wait another day, you can't change your ticket," he said. "But we'll do our best to get you over to Kingston."

Born to Preach

When I arrived back in Corpus, I soon learned why God wanted me to return early. My pastor's wife, Anna Salstrand, was dying from breast cancer.

If I had delayed my return any longer, I would have missed spending time with this precious woman who had so touched and influenced my life.

A soft-spoken redhead, Anna had always dressed in white when she preached. Whereas her husband shouted at people in his preaching, she was the one who spiritually fed the congregation with her quiet strength. A prayer warrior and intercessor, she spent hours in the sanctuary interceding at the altar. In church services, if she wasn't in the pulpit preaching, she was on the front row praying for the person who was.

If ever I patterned myself after anyone, it would have been Sister Salstrand. She had been my mentor at Corpus Christi Tabernacle, and I loved and admired her. I was very sad to lose her.

The Salstrand family was devastated by her loss. To help out, I stayed and preached in the church for another week after her passing.

❧❦

During those several weeks back in Corpus, I suffered a problem with internal bleeding and had to see a doctor. Following an examination, the doctor asked, "Have you had your appendix removed?"

"No," I replied.

Chapter 6: A Leap of Faith

"Well, you definitely don't have an appendix, but you do have an *internal* scar where it would have been."

Later, I remembered the touch of God that I had experienced in my body at T.L. Osborn's healing meeting back in my teens. It seemed this doctor had confirmed that my troublesome appendix had been removed but evidently not by the hands of man. The Lord continued to show me His faithfulness.

I left town once more, this time with an invitation to preach in Indianapolis. God had promised me that, if I trusted Him, He would open doors of ministry for me. I was still alone, but traveling was easier now that I had quit feeling sorry for myself and trusted God with His plan for my life. And doors were indeed opening.

The church in Indianapolis graciously provided an apartment above the sanctuary for me, and after breakfast each day I remained inside and spent time in prayer. The Lord began speaking to me on my second morning there.

Daughter, you have been single and you have walked alone, but you're not going to walk alone anymore, He said. *I am going to give you someone who will walk by your side, hold your hand, and share the joys and sorrows of the ministry with you.*

I had my eyes closed as the Lord spoke, but it seemed as if I saw another person standing right beside me.

That same night after the service, the pastor's wife told me she had a word for me. "Come in the office and I'll tell you about it," she said. "It's personal and I wouldn't prophesy this in front of the church but I know it's from God."

"Well, please tell me more," I replied.

"You're single because you live what you preach," she began. "You've walked alone, but you're not going to walk alone any longer. God's going to bring somebody into your life. You're going to fall in love and marry, and it's going to be sooner than you think."

Her words were almost exactly the same as those spoken to me that very morning. I knew it was a divine confirmation.

"If I never see you again, I don't need to know whether this comes to pass or not," she declared, "because I know this is the word of the Lord."

❧

But darkness, too, was at work. It seemed like the Enemy was trying to undermine God's plans and my faith in His promises.

The next morning, I was alone in the little church apartment when I heard a knock on the door. When I opened it, there stood the pastor—a stocky, balding, red-haired man in his late forties. For several moments we stood in the doorway making small talk. Then, all of a sudden, he grabbed my wrist and tried to push the door open.

In one rapid motion, I yanked my hand free and shoved the door shut. I'd never had anything like that happen before, and I was shaken to the core. Several minutes went by before I could stop trembling. When I felt somewhat calm again, I wondered if I could—or should—preach that night. Only after praying through the afternoon did I feel settled enough to handle the service.

The next morning the pastor's wife, who also led another congregation in a nearby town, phoned. When she heard my voice she said, "I don't know what's happened, but you're not the same."

I didn't want to say anything about my encounter with her husband, but she was persistent. She wanted to meet in the church office. "I want to know what's wrong," she insisted. "I know something's happened."

She had treated me kindly, and so I finally told her what had transpired. She quickly picked up the phone and called her husband. When he denied everything, her attitude towards me changed abruptly. "We heard all about you before you ever came here," she said sarcastically.

"Really?" I asked calmly. "I'd like to know precisely what you've heard. I know there are no skeletons in my closet."

The woman tried to intimidate me with her words and threats. "I don't have to sit here and listen to this," I said wearily. "I'll preach tonight's service but it will be my last. I'll be leaving tomorrow."

In retrospect I surmised that pastor had been guilty of indiscretions before. I believed his wife knew about his life out of the pulpit and was actually covering his lies.

Years before I entered the ministry, the Lord had quickened to me the truths of Romans 6:13, where we are exhorted to yield our "members as instruments of righteousness unto God" (KJV).

Watch your reputation and keep your life clean, He instructed me. *If you do not, it will come back and hurt you and the ministry I have entrusted to you.*

Born to Preach

I lived by those scriptures and the words of God's instruction. I knew there could be no gray areas in my life or ministry. So when I was accused of having an unsavory reputation, I was able to let it go and move on.

I had nothing to hide.

Anne as a baby.

Anne at 6 years old with
her sister.

Anne at 5 years old.

Anne's father broadcasting
at KXYZ in Houston.

Anne with her older sister.

Mom & Dad,
Pauline & Charles.

With Granddaughter Amelia.

Ordained as Bishop
of RMF, May 2008.

In Fiji.

Bishop Anne's return to the pulpit.

Chapter 7
A Man Named John

Evangelist
ANNE E. NETHERY

Photo that John saw and said
"I'm going to marry that girl!"

Born to Preach

Chapter 7

A Man Named John

"God sovereignly invades the circumstances of our lives at times with what we might call 'coincidence'. Yet, when one gains a different perspective on the so-called 'coincidence', it's not some random event at all. It's the sovereign hand of God."

—Anne Gimenez

I was living my dream now and doing what I loved—traveling from city to city and church to church preaching the Gospel. Like most single women, I sometimes would wonder if marriage was in my future. Considering my constant travel, however, I had to ask myself, "How will I ever find time to get to know someone well enough to marry?" I decided to leave that problem to God.

One day, while preaching in the Pittsburgh area, I received a phone call from an old friend, Bea Lamont. I had first met this lively, outgoing preacher several years earlier while holding services in the same area.

I was thrilled to hear her voice again. We chatted a few moments and then she asked pointedly, "Where will you be next Monday?"

"I'll be staying overnight in South Bend, Indiana," I answered, "on my way to Ypsilanti, Michigan, where I'm to preach for a week." I had planned to stop in South Bend to pick up some stationary I had ordered for my radio program in Corpus.

"Good! I'll plan to meet you there!" she replied enthusiastically. "I want to take you to a service at Calvary Temple. A group called The Addicts will be performing there, and you just *have* to hear their testimony!"

Bea went on to tell me how this group—whom she referred to as "the boys"—was traveling the country, singing and giving their testimonies of being delivered from drugs. They had ministered in her church, and she praised them highly. Clearly, she was "hooked" on them.

But I had little interest in meeting a team of former drug addicts. The only thing I knew about people with drug problems was what I'd read in *The Saturday Evening Post*.

Bea was certain it was no coincidence that I planned to be in South Bend the same night "the boys" would be ministering there. So determined was she to introduce me to her new friends that she drove the 300 miles from Pittsburgh to South Bend to make sure I went to the service.

When we arrived at Calvary Temple, we were immediately ushered to two reserved seats on the front row. Perhaps I should have suspected something then, but I took Bea at her word—she wanted me to hear the testimonies of her new friends.

The program went as expected until the third act. When the curtain rose, I saw a dark, heavy-set man. His dirty tee-shirt revealed a potbelly, and his hair was disheveled and sprayed almost white. He was acting the part of a drunken policeman.

Bea punched me. "There's your future husband!" she whispered.

I was not impressed, and I chose not to respond. *I'm single, but I'm not desperate,* I thought to myself.

After the play concluded, I started to walk out with Bea. "Let's wait a minute," she said. "I want you to meet some of the boys."

The leader of the group, John Gimenez, and several of the other men walked over to greet Bea, and she introduced me to each one. "Nice to meet you," I responded repeatedly, offering my hand half-heartedly to each one.

Bea was determined the evening would not end early. "Are you boys hungry?" she asked. Without waiting for a reply, she quickly added, "Let's go get a hamburger!" I didn't want to go anywhere with these people; I simply wanted to go back to the hotel. I frankly didn't care to know these Addicts any better.

"Johnny can ride with us and we'll drop him off at the pastor's house later," Bea continued. "Some other folks can bring the rest of the guys."

We got into my car and drove to a nearby restaurant. As we waited to order, we engaged in some light conversation. It seemed to me that John disagreed with everything I said. It was like rubbing a cat's fur the wrong way.

Finally, I told myself, "Just be quiet, and eat your hamburger. This will soon be over and you can get away from these people."

Later, as we drove John to the pastor's house where he was staying, he and Bea kept up a continual light-hearted chatter. Suddenly, Bea stopped and asked, "Anne Nethery, why do you have that man's hat sitting in the back window ledge of your car?"

When I had first begun to travel at night, I had placed that hat back there for protection. I wanted it to look as if a man were in my car with me.

Instead of telling Bea the real reason, however, I laughed. "You've heard the Cinderella story about the glass slipper," I answered. "Well, I'm gonna marry the man who can wear that hat." I laughed and laughed at my own joke.

I thought *nobody* could wear that large a hat. But when I glanced in the rearview mirror, John had it on. It was a perfect fit. Unbelievable.

❧

The next morning I had breakfast with Bea, John and several of "the boys." It was pleasant, but it was a relief to say goodbye at last and head to Ypsilanti.

As I drove off, I told the Lord. "I don't ever want to see those people again...I'll be good for the rest of my days if You'll keep me away from them."

The first service in Ypsilanti was in a small country church outside of town. I was about a third of the way into my message when the back door opened, and in walked four of The Addicts, all wearing dark overcoats and fedora hats. Bea Lamont was with them.

Chapter 7: A Man Named John

To those sitting in the pews, it must have looked like the mafia had found me!

I had to stop the service because of all the commotion. When order was finally restored, I introduced Bea, and she promptly turned the service over to The Addicts. They gave their testimonies and sang, and the pastor took up an offering for the team.

Afterwards, when they left for Pennsylvania, I thought I'd finally gotten rid of everybody. The next morning at the pastor's home, however, I was awakened by a ringing phone. It was Bea.

"We've driven all night and gotten lost several times. Believe it or not but we're still in Ypsilanti." she said happily. "We're getting ready to eat and I've sent my niece to pick you up to have breakfast with us. Then, we're definitely leaving for Pittsburgh."

When I got to the restaurant, the only empty seat was beside John. As we chatted that morning, I asked, "Do you speak Spanish?"

"Sure," he replied.

"Well, say something to me in Spanish," I suggested. John responded with a blank stare.

"I know something in Spanish," I said impulsively. "*Yo te amo con todo mi corazón.*"

John's dark eyes got huge. His reaction shocked me. I had simply repeated a phrase my former boyfriend, Waymond, had taught me: "I love you with all my heart."

Did he think I meant it? I thought to myself. *What an idiot!*

"What'd she say…what'd she say?" one of the guys asked John. He just shook his head, refusing to answer.

❧

After completing the meetings in Ypsilanti, I left for Detroit. There, just before the first night's service, I received a phone call from my sister. She was four months pregnant and doctors had just discovered she had cancer.

"I'm going in tomorrow for another pap smear and tests," she explained, "and by the end of the week they'll possibly do a complete hysterectomy. The doctors are saying it may save my life."

Shaken to the core at Beverly's news, I walked into my hotel room, raised my hands and declared, "Lord, Your Word says if I abide in Your Word and Your Word abides in me, I can ask and it will be given me, and I ask for my sister's life."

That night, I wept all the way to church over my sister's condition. I even told the Lord I couldn't preach that night. "I've preached when I've been scared, hurt and sick," I tried to explain, "but I can't preach tonight."

In the midst of my struggles, a song emerged from my heart and brought peace. *Stand up, Paul, and dry up your tears… You must preach the Gospel for many long years.*

I had just come in from that night's service when the phone rang once again. This time, it was John. He was in Chester Springs, Pennsylvania, making a film about The Addicts. He had gotten my phone number from Bea. I told him about my sister's problem and then and there he prayed for her—and me.

Chapter 7: A Man Named John

Every night that week, John called after eleven o'clock to check on me and ask about my sister. To our great relief, by the end of the week, doctors had successfully operated on Beverly. She was going to make it.

At the end of two weeks, John and I had talked an hour every night, and I began to think of him as a good friend. "I don't know how to tell you this," John volunteered one night, "but I think something's going to happen between you and me."

I laughed. "John, I've had plenty of guys tell me that before."

But through our late-night phone conversations, our friendship continued to develop. He called frequently and told me what he was doing and asked about my family. My family didn't call at all, and I was with strangers in a different church each week. Thus, his phone calls became a little thread of normalcy for me.

Then John invited me to join him at the movie set in Chester Springs, so I could watch the filming of *Way Out* and meet some of his family and old friends from New York.

By this time, he was saying he wanted to marry me. He also had a confession to make. "When I saw your picture the first time, it was at Bea Lamont's office, "and she told me about you."

"Well, that's news to me," I replied.

"I told her I was gonna marry you," John said. "She told me, 'Fat chance you've got, fella'!" We both couldn't help but laugh over the exchange.

❧

When Bea came for a visit, John asked her to help me pick out an engagement ring. She did, and it was beautiful. I happily wore it when I returned home to Corpus a few weeks later.

After completing the film, John and The Addicts crisscrossed America for almost a year. Three teams traveled in three separate vans, performing in churches, schools, clubs, and Full Gospel Businessmen's chapters, all across the land.

Once, I was in a service with The Addicts in a Williamsport, Pennsylvania, church. There was little anointing on the team's efforts, and John, sensing something was wrong, eventually stopped the service and called for prayer. The pastor then walked back to where I was sitting and asked if I would take the service.

"I believe the Lord wants us to lift up each one of these guys in prayer," I announced. Then, the pastor and I began to lay hands on each member of the team and pray.

When we approached John, I held back, hoping the pastor would pray. Several moments passed, and then I reluctantly placed my hands on John's head and prophesied.

I have brought thee forth from a pit and I have put My Spirit in thee, but thou hast forsaken Me. Thus, I will strip thee and make thee as one who is naked. But I again shall build thee and what is built will be of Me.

In a matter of months, the prophecy came true. The delicate thread that held the teams together snapped and began to unravel. Some of the men slipped, dabbled in drugs, and then backslid. The travel vans were soon repossessed and The Addicts scattered—many of them going back to the streets from which they had come.

John, the team's leader, fared no better. He, too, seemed to be caught in an overwhelming undertow that threatened to drag him back into his old lifestyle. At first, he put up a good fight.

Chapter 7: A Man Named John

He enrolled in Elim Bible Institute in Lima, New York, and for a year, struggled through the classes, causing problems for himself, his teachers and his classmates. John's once active ministry came to a dead stop.

Overcome by his old habits and rebellion, he reached a point where he was barely surviving off the helping hand of a tender-hearted pastor by the name of David Minor in Coudersport, Pennsylvania. Brother Minor reached out to John when John had no place else to go.

I knew Brother Minor, having preached services for him, and I tearfully sought his counsel about John.

Throughout this trying time, it seemed my mother was always telling me about somebody else she knew of, who would make a good husband. She even told one of her sisters, "We've got to pray she won't marry this guy."

"Let's pray the will of the Lord be done," my Aunt Ruby countered.

"No, no, no," Mother answered. "Let's pray she won't marry *this* man."

In years past, I had been in several relationships but had walked away from each one. Once, my mother and I had even traveled to California on a brief vacation to attend some church services and visit a pastor I was interested in.

Yet on the train headed back home, the words of 1 Corinthians 2:9 came to mind. "*...Eye has not seen, nor ear heard, nor have entered into the heart of man, the things which God has prepared for those who love Him*" (NKJV).

And I heard the Lord saying simply, *This is not what I have prepared for you.*

I had learned to look to God as my matchmaker, and I now cried out to Him in desperation about John Gimenez. "All I want You to tell me, Lord, is either yes or no," I frequently prayed. I never heard an answer to that particular prayer.

❦

By August 1, 1967, almost thirty months had passed since I first met John in South Bend. As I watched the disastrous spiral enveloping his life, I continued to intercede for him. Then, late one night he called. He was in trouble and asked if I'd come to New York City to get him. At the time, I was at Elim in Lima, New York.

With the aid of Louis, a friend of John's, and a former addict himself, I drove from Lima into the Bronx to look for him. Miraculously, we managed to locate John's old territory of "Korea" and began driving up and down Westchester Avenue, across Simpson Street and down Fox Street, searching for him.

At one intersection, I stopped for a red light and noticed a darkened figure staggering across the street. Fear grabbed at my heart as I stared at the stumbling man. Could it be?

It was John!

Louis and I jumped out of the car and piled the thin, spaghetti-legged creature into the backseat. He was high, his eyes bleary and bloodshot, his words slurred.

"When we gonna get married, babe?" he mumbled.

Chapter 7: A Man Named John

I kept my eyes riveted on the road and drove on without answering.

"You know I love you, don'tcha?"

"Yeah, sure you do," I replied coldly.

"No, I mean it…I really do…no kiddin.'"

He irritated me to the core, but I stayed calm and kept my eyes on the road. I felt I'd had all of John Gimenez I could take.

"Well, how 'bout it?" John pressed again. "When we gonna get married?"

I continued to ignore him and plowed down the road that led out of New York and into Pennsylvania. Highway 84 soon became U.S. 6. It was past midnight and Coudersport was still four hours away. I prayed silently that the time would pass quickly. By now, I felt I wanted nothing more than to drop John off and get him out of my life.

"Well, I'm waitin,'" John persisted.

To get him to cease his badgering, I answered quietly, "In about a month."

The answer seemed to pacify him and he dropped off to sleep, as did his friend Louis. About six o'clock in the morning, I pulled up to David Minor's white clapboard house in Coudersport, and dropped John and Louis off. After a hurried breakfast, Brother Minor's daughter Sharon and I departed for a large camp meeting in New Brunswick, Canada. I never intended to look back.

The night before the camp meeting ended, however, John telephoned. I didn't even want to take the call when I was told he was on the phone. Reluctantly, I picked up the receiver. "Anne, I've had a real meeting with God," he said softly.

I could tell by the sound of his voice that something *was* different. "What happened?" I asked.

"I was staying on the third floor of Brother Minor's house," John began, "and I'm not sure if I was awake or having a dream. But I saw bars surrounding me and I was lying on a bed with a decomposing corpse beside me. God told me I had never gotten out of bed with my old man—the past. I literally screamed and screamed until I was hoarse."

"That's great, John," I said, pleased that he had heard from God but still skeptical.

"I've *never* had a meeting with God like that before," he continued. "It's done something for me, and I want to see you when you get back."

The following Monday, Sharon and I left New Brunswick and drove all the way back, dropping off one of the girls at Elim, and arriving in Coudersport about ten o'clock that night. They told me John was upstairs, so I went up and knocked on his door.

When I looked into his face, I knew that God *had* done something supernatural in John's life. His eyes told me the story; they were bright and clear. In fact, his whole countenance had changed.

John went over the entire story with me. When he finished, he said, "Anne, we've talked about getting married for two and a half years. If that's not what we're going to do, let's just forget it. I believe it's either now or never."

Chapter 7: A Man Named John

I knew that marriage to John Gimenez would mean total rejection from my family, but I decided that night I wanted to spend the rest of my life with him—even though he'd only been "clean" from drugs for one month.

"It's now," I told him. "It's now." And we sealed our words with a kiss.

❧

Brother Minor had some reservations about performing the service and said he needed to pray about his decision. That was Monday night, and by Wednesday he gave us his consent. "I'm ready to get you folks married if you're still asking," he volunteered.

Meanwhile, I was still doing some praying on my own. I've never advocated that people randomly open the Bible looking for a word to guide them, but frankly that's what I did—not once but three times.

The first time, John 1:6 practically leaped off the page in front of me. *"There was a man sent from God, whose name was John"* (NKJV).

The second time I opened the Bible, I was looking at Acts 10:15, *"...What God hath cleansed, that call not thou common"* (NKJV).

The third time, my eyes looked straight at Esther 4:14, *"...and who knoweth whether thou art come to the kingdom for such a time as this?"* (KJV).

Encouraged by those scriptures and by Brother Minor's prayers and commitment to do the ceremony, John and I got a marriage license and prepared for our wedding on Friday night.

Thursday night I telephoned my brother-in-law, Dick Campbell, announcing that I was getting married the following night. "Tomorrow night around eight, you tell my folks I'm married and I'll call them in a day or so," I instructed.

Dick reluctantly agreed to the assignment but later panicked, fearing his in-laws would blame him for the belated news. So he called and informed them of our plans. Within minutes, my parents telephoned me. I did my best to explain my decision to them, but nothing helped.

Fully aware of John's problems—both past and present—my parents were dead set against the marriage.

The conversation, calm at first, grew heated. "If you go through with this…if you walk down that aisle and stand in front of that preacher, you'll never see my face again," my mother warned, "and I'll be cursing your marriage."

"Oh, Mother, I've lived single thirty-four years, almost thirty-five, and I can live another thirty-five or so if God wants me to," I suggested.

"Well, why don't you marry a *white* man then?" was her sarcastic reply.

Having been raised in a Texas town near the Mexican border, I understood but did not condone my parents' feelings. John's physical features—olive complexion, black hair, dark eyes—reflected his Puerto Rican ancestry. Plus, he spoke Spanish. My family identified all of those attributes as Mexican, and in their town—and in that day—Mexicans stood last in the social order.

John finally walked into the kitchen and saw my tears and my hand shaking as I tried to hold onto the phone. "Hang up," he urged. "Hang up."

I shook my head "no" and covered the mouthpiece with my hand. "No, they have a right to what they're saying," I mumbled. "They believe they're trying to save my life."

I was dispirited when the conversation ended, but also determined to follow what I believed was God's direction for my life—and John's. "Don't worry," he told me. "You're not a child and I'm not either. We know what we're doing. They have their lives to live and we do too."

Brother Minor further soothed my troubled heart by offering some sage advice. "Sister, the Bible simply says to honor father and mother," he reminded me. "I believe you've done that…now we just have to leave the rest to God."

The wedding date arrived—September 1, 1967—the Friday before Labor Day. Most of our friends couldn't attend since our wedding had been planned so hurriedly, but my friend from Elim, Sara Bright, came down to be maid-of-honor and John's friend, David Hunter, served as best man.

I didn't have a wedding dress for the ceremony, so I planned to wear a white suit that I'd often preached in. I would carry my Bible along with an orchid a friend had kindly provided. I was dressed and ready to go downstairs when panic hit me and I thought, *Oh, God, what am I doing?*

For several agonizing minutes, I wrestled with my fears. Finally, I confessed, "God, if this is a mistake, it's the most honest one I've ever made. And if I'm wrong, I believe You'll turn a curse into a blessing."

With my peace restored, I descended the stairs to the basement of the old clapboard house, where Brother Minor's church met.

Born to Preach

When I finally arrived for the ceremony, the wedding march had already been played three times. John had begun to think I'd gotten cold feet and wasn't coming. He was very nearly right.

Throughout the ceremony, we stood before Brother Minor with tears streaming down our faces. As we knelt and heard his prayer over our future lives together, God's presence was so precious and so near. We were weeping softly as the service concluded.

Chapter 8
Marriage & A New Life

John and Anne's wedding,
September 1, 1967

Born to Preach

Chapter 8

Marriage & A New Life

"Marriage is a joyous occasion. It is connected in our thoughts with the charm of home and with all that is pleasant and attractive in the tenderest and most sacred relations of life."

—*from a traditional Wedding Ceremony*

We spent our honeymoon in Hartford, Connecticut, a historic city I'd enjoyed visiting before. While we were there, we stopped off at the Hartford Revival Center where I had previously held meetings. After the service, Pastor Sands rushed up to us. "Oh, thank God, you're here," he enthused. "You're an answer to prayer.

"What?" I said, not understanding.

"You're the answer to my prayer," he explained. "I've got a visiting preacher who's killing this revival and I need your help."

"Well, we *are* on a honeymoon," I said hesitantly. "We just came by for a visit."

"What about it?" the preacher continued.

"That's up to John," I said. "If he thinks it's okay, I'll preach."

"Yeah, sure," John agreed pleasantly. "Go ahead."

I preached the remainder of that week's revival, and then we drove back to Coudersport, stopping off briefly at a retreat in Mountaindale, New York, where John and many of The Addicts' team members had first come following their conversions.

When we were first married, we lived in a tiny, $50-a-month apartment near Brother Minor's church. John helped support us by painting houses with Brother Minor, and I occasionally preached in various places nearby. But after John nearly fell off a roof, we decided his services could be better utilized elsewhere without endangering his health.

About three months after our wedding, officials at Elim Bible Institute contacted John about helping with a large outdoor crusade in Bogotá, Colombia. His ability to speak Spanish would be a great asset to their team.

I had now been in full-time ministry for over four years, and God had always spoken to me firsthand about ventures of faith. I hadn't heard anything about going to South America, and told John so.

"I think we're going," John responded simply.

"We'll see," I said with a shrug.

Since Elim wasn't helping with our expenses, we began seeking missionary offerings to pay for the trip. The necessary funds arrived in good time, but our passports and tickets did not come through until the day before we were to leave. Even when all was in order for our departure, I was still unsure we were to go.

Then, the morning of our departure, I awoke early and heard the Lord say, *You are going.*

Chapter 8: Marriage & a New Life

It suddenly occurred to me that John had been right all along. Now that I was a married woman, I had to realize that God wouldn't always speak to me before He spoke to John. When he awoke, I told John what the Lord had said and confessed my wrong attitude.

Throughout the early days of marriage, we had to learn to flow together as one instead of two. Once, at a gathering of preachers in Peoria, Illinois, John decided at the last minute that he wanted me to say something before he gave his testimony.

I had been told the group was a meeting of *evangelical* pastors and I just presumed they were all Pentecostals. I greeted them with a hearty "Praise the Lord! God's moving by His Spirit in all the earth!"

Most of them just stared at me, expressionless. I thought, *It's early in the morning. They must be half-asleep.*

I continued, "It's just like Joel said; He's pouring out His Spirit upon all the earth! Great things are happening today!"

Now, some of them were glaring at me. A few even yawned. *Boy, this is the deadest group of Pentecostal preachers I've ever seen,* I thought. *I need to rear back and find something to move 'em.*

"We just heard the other day that 46 Catholics at Notre Dame got filled with the Holy Ghost," I yelled out, "and they're speaking with other tongues as the Spirit of God gives utterance!"

From his seat on the front row, John was inwardly cringing. Later he told me he thought to himself, *She's either crazy or doesn't have any idea who she's speaking to.*

Finally, the truth dawned on me—we weren't among like-minded, Sprit-filled brothers—and I quickly took my seat. "Get me out of here as fast as you can," I muttered to John. He did.

As plans developed for the trip to South America, I had many opportunities to say, "I told you this wasn't God." But I was learning to trust God to lead John and knew I needed to hold back from making such comments.

⇛⇝

We did encounter some logistical problems on the trip—airline delays, missing luggage, hotel mix-ups. After flying from Miami to Barranquilla, Colombia, what was supposed to be a two hour layover for a flight to Bogotá turned into six hours. Even worse, when we finally arrived, the airline couldn't locate John's luggage.

While the airline staff searched for it, John paced back and forth in the baggage area. All at once, he spotted a tall, seedy looking man carrying his bright plaid suitcase. John ran after the man, shouting, "Give me my suitcase!"

The startled man dropped the bag and fled, and John quickly scooped everything up. The claim ticket had been popped from the luggage but all of John's clothes—including the two new suits I'd bought for him—were safe inside.

Finally, we arrived in Bogotá and checked into the hotel at nightfall. We were both bone-tired from our travels, and wanted nothing more than to get some rest. An attendant escorted us to a room, which I quickly noted had two twin beds. John didn't seem to mind, but I did. "Ask the attendant if he has a room with a double bed," I said, letting John know I wasn't happy.

He looked surprised. "I'm not asking him that," he said sheepishly. "What'll he think?" He glanced over at the attendant standing beside the baggage cart, watching us.

"I don't care what he thinks," I replied. "It's fifty degrees outside and there's only a sheet and a bedspread on those beds...I'm not sleeping by myself."

With that, John turned to the man and explained in Spanish that we were newlyweds. The man looked at me, then back at John and grinned. Within a few minutes, he had found a room with a comfortable double bed.

❧❧

The next morning John phoned Carlton Spencer, an Elim official who was already in Bogotá to help with the crusade. "We're here," he announced excitedly.

"You're here?" Carlton responded. "What do you mean you're here? Didn't you get the letter?"

Now it was John's turn to be surprised. "What letter?" he asked.

"We wrote telling you not to come. There were problems with the crusade and we've had to cancel. We're just here trying to work out the details of rescheduling the event."

John was crestfallen. He hung up the phone and reluctantly told me the story. "You might have been right all along," he admitted.

"Maybe so, but why don't we just wait a few days," I suggested. In fact, I hoped I *hadn't* been right, for John's sake.

John nodded. "I guess so. There's no need in trying to catch the first plane back to the States. We're here and might as well spend a few days."

"I'm tired anyway," I confessed. "I'd like to rest a couple of days. Maybe God'll do something."

The temperature in Bogotá averages about 58 degrees year round. It's something like being in an "air conditioned" city at an altitude of 8,600 feet. We spent a day sightseeing as well as trying to dodge most of Bogotá's pickpockets and frantic taxi drivers.

The next day we were invited to a missionary retreat, *La Mesa*, located in a small town back in the Andes Mountains, where we spent several days. Then, two days before Christmas, John felt the Lord speaking to him. *Go back to the city.*

Our return to Bogotá proved to be the blessing of the Lord. When we walked into the tiny hotel lobby in Bogotá, Johnny Isles, a young missionary acquaintance I'd known from the States, was checking out.

We exchanged greetings with Johnny and he introduced us to Hector Pardo, a Colombian pastor, who was driving him to the airport. When the pastor heard we were ministers, he insisted that we hold services in his church. Those meetings proved that God had been ordering our steps all along.

When Hector publicized the fact that "Reverend Gimenez" would be at his church, people throughout Bogotá thought "Reverend Gimenez" was the well-known Puerto Rican evangelist whose name sounded the same as ours but was spelled "Jimenez." When we arrived the first night, the church was packed out.

John had taught me some scripture choruses in Spanish, so we sang and I kept the beat with my trusty tambourine. Often, I preached in English, and John interpreted. He also gave his amazing testimony. The people loved it, and best of all, God blessed his delivery.

Churches throughout the city opened their doors to us, and crowds followed us from one church to another, jamming into buildings so that lines extended to the sidewalks. The power of God was manifested in many physical healings and miracles. One elderly man's deformed hand was miraculously restored as John prayed, and hundreds were saved.

❧❧

Elim invited us to stay at a large apartment with five bedrooms, which was set aside for the crusade. At the time, Sixto Lopez, a former missionary to Cuba who now had a radio ministry in Bogotá, was also lodging there.

Sixto casually mentioned one afternoon that Pat Robertson, founder of the Christian Broadcasting Network, would be in Bogotá soon to negotiate the purchase of a radio station.

John smiled at the prospect of seeing Pat again. He had met him, as well as Demos Shakarian, back in 1965 during a Full Gospel Businessmen's airlift to London. During that trip, John's team of Addicts had led many drug users from the Soho district to Christ. He and Pat had also appeared on television together in England talking about the Soho conversions.

Sure enough, Pat arrived in a few days, and he and John quickly resumed their friendship. Pat vividly remembered their introduction in London and the revival among the Soho drug users. After finalizing his business in Bogotá, he made preparations to return home.

"Whenever you're back in the States, get in touch with me," he told John over lunch one day. "There's a genuine revival going on in Tidewater, Virginia, and I'd like to have you as a guest on the 700 Club."

"Sure," John gladly agreed.

Neither of us had any idea of how God was even now orchestrating our lives and future. Only in looking back would we recognize the importance of that simple invitation. It was prophetic!

What was supposed to have been a brief stay in Bogotá turned into six weeks of extended ministry. At the end of January 1968, we returned to the States. We both had scheduled speaking dates in Texas—together in San Antonio, then separately, with John in Houston and me in Corpus Christi.

I desperately wished that John could visit my family in Corpus Christi, but my parents' hostile attitude toward our marriage hadn't changed. Mother continued to address all letters to me using my maiden name. "I'll never acknowledge that you're married," she wrote.

The strain was overwhelming. At times, it felt like a stabbing pain in my heart that wouldn't go away. Many nights I lay awake—unable to sleep because of the stress. "If I could get just one prayer answered, Lord," I prayed continually, "I'd like to have this situation resolved with my family."

While we were in San Antonio, John reached a decision. "I'm not going to force myself on your family," he said. "I won't go down there and *make* them meet me. I'll travel to Houston, and then I can fly down to Corpus. We'll trade in our car as we planned, do the speaking dates in Orange, and go back to Pennsylvania."

Chapter 8: Marriage & a New Life

I agreed. We did a week of meetings in San Antonio, and then I drove to Corpus Christi while John flew to Houston. I stayed with my best friend, JoEllen Forbus, and I telephoned my parents once I got to Corpus. Later I visited briefly, showing them photographs of the trip to South America.

As I prepared to go, my father surprised me by issuing an invitation. "Since you're in town, why don't you come over and spend Wednesday night?"

"Okay, if that's what you want," I answered.

"Sure we do," he smiled, emphasizing the "we." My mother was quiet.

I preached that Wednesday night at my old church, then drove to my parents' house. When I reached the front door, my father was there waiting for me. "Hurry, hurry," he said excitedly. "John's on the radio."

I was puzzled. *He must mean John's calling on the telephone,* I thought, following my dad into a back bedroom. Mother lay across a bed listening to the sound of John's voice over her FM radio.

"I didn't know John was going to be on the radio," I volunteered.

"Sh-sh-sh-sh-sh," my parents insisted.

For another hour or so, we sat listening intently to John's testimony. I marveled at what God seemed to be doing. Somehow my mother, in turning the radio dial, had picked up the signal beaming John's voice from station KPRC in Houston—240 miles away. When she heard the name "Gimenez", she turned back to listen. Then, the Holy Spirit went to work.

Born to Preach

John's appearance on the radio show had been arranged by the pastor of the church in Houston, where he was preaching. He shared briefly how God had delivered him from drug addiction, how the Lord was blessing his life, and how God had worked miracles during our just-completed trip to South America.

As John spoke, the telephone in the studio began to ring. So many people had questions for him that he was allowed to continue past his allotted time. When nine o'clock came, the radio station's power was boosted, so that its signal reached a circle with a radius of a full two hundred miles. That circle now included Corpus Christi—and John's in-laws.

"Here's a fairly hot question," the announcer warned John. "You've been talking about how God handles problems. Do you have any problems or trials that aren't solved?"

John took a deep breath. "Yeah, sure I have problems," he began. "In fact, I'm in the middle of one right now. My wife is in Corpus Christi visiting her parents. They don't want me to visit them. I'm Puerto Rican and an ex-drug addict and they feel their daughter has made a big mistake in marrying somebody like me.

"That hurts for somebody to be prejudiced against me. Yet when I look at the situation closer, I realize I might feel the same way if my daughter married a guy who'd been a dope fiend from New York. I'd probably be upset too. So I do have problems...and a few testings as well.

"But I believe that the day will come when my in-laws realize I love them and we'll be a family together. They'll see I genuinely love their daughter and mean her no harm—only good. I've never met them, but I understand how they can feel the way they do; and I'll love and respect them no matter what."

A warm glow rose inside me as I listened to John's heart-rending words. Miracles were underway. God was at work—and I could feel it.

The next morning my mother brought up the subject of John's coming to get me. She spoke hesitantly. "It's your father's idea," she emphasized. "When John comes down here—by the way, when is he coming?"

"He'll fly down on Friday," I answered. "We're trading in my old car and then we're leaving on Monday."

"Well, your father wants you to bring him to the house," she mumbled.

"That's fine," I beamed.

My sister and her husband, Dick Campbell, accompanied me to the airport, where we picked up a feverish John Gimenez. For several weeks, he had been plagued by a flu bug, his immune system perhaps weakened by our travels.

When we arrived at the Campbell's house and were seated in their living room, he announced, "I'm really worn out and feeling a little light-headed. I think I'll rest a while before supper."

Up to this point, Beverly had been rather cold toward John. Like our mother, she had condemned my marriage for months. Once, she had even written me a caustic letter implying I had done something evil in marrying a converted former drug addict. "Look what you've done to us," she wrote bitterly.

But now, faced with a less-than-healthy John, she became genuinely concerned over his condition. "What's the matter, John?" she asked gently. "Is there anything we can do?"

"I don't know—maybe pray," he suggested weakly. "I've just had this flu awhile and can't seem to shake it."

Suddenly, the Presence of the Lord filled the room and Beverly sprang out of her chair, speaking in tongues. John said later he felt like he'd been struck by lightning when she laid hands on him. Healing came instantly as all his symptoms vanished.

That miracle ended Beverly's opposition to John. Later, over a meal at a Chinese restaurant, Beverly and Dick planned how we could handle things at our parents' house if John's visit with them turned out badly. But our plans were unnecessary. God had still more miracles in store.

When the four of us arrived at my parents' house, Daddy was standing in the doorway, holding the screen door open and wearing a wide smile on his face. "John, I heard you on the radio the other night," he announced warmly, clasping his son-in-law's hand in a firm grip. Mother acted graciously too.

God had sovereignly used the radio program to break down my parents' walls of fear and generational lines of prejudice. Through His compassionate touch, the Lord honored a prophetic word my friend had spoken to me just a few days before.

While I was still in San Antonio, before coming to Corpus, an old friend had brought me an encouraging word. "You are God's child and He loves you," she assured me. "He's going to do something you want very much…and it's going to be very quick too."

Just as she prophesied, God answered the prayers of my heart.

Chapter 9
Women Preachers

Singing on The 700 Club, 1968

Chapter 9

Women Preachers

"There is [now no distinction] neither Jew nor Greek, there is neither slave nor free, there is not male and female; for you are all one in Christ Jesus."

—Galatians 3:28 (Amplified Bible)

Orange, the easternmost city in Texas, is located on the Sabine River at the border with Louisiana. That's where we held our last meeting before returning to Coudersport. The first two nights, John preached by himself so I could make a quick trip to Hartford for a conference at Brother Sands' church. I flew back to Texas to join him for the final night of services.

About an hour before the service was to begin, there was a knock on our motel door. I was taking a shower, so John went to the door and opened it. Two of the church elders were standing there. "Ah, I don't really know how to put all this," one of them ventured, looking rather uncomfortable.

"Well, just go ahead and say it the best you can," John responded.

"Okay," he agreed. "The pastor wanted us to come over and tell you that he wants you to give your testimony tonight but your wife is not to speak from the pulpit."

John gave me the news when I got out of the shower. "Evidently these people don't believe in a woman having a ministry," he fumed, his temper rising.

"Obviously not."

"I'm calling the preacher and canceling the meeting," John decided.

"Wait a minute," I said. "Put the phone down."

He stopped dialing, thought for a moment, and then placed the receiver back in its cradle.

"This man didn't put me in the ministry and he's not going to take me out," I explained. "If we leave, he'll just say we can't be relied upon."

"What do you suggest doing then?" he asked, turning to look at me.

"Well, they've made it plain I'm not welcome, so I won't go to church tonight," I concluded. "You go ahead though and do whatever God leads you to do."

He was quiet for a few moments. "You're probably right," he said finally, "but I still don't like it."

That night, John responded to the pastor's request to give his personal testimony. He took his listeners into the depths of his sixteen years of drug addiction…the pain, the sorrow, the heartbreak. People throughout the church wept openly as he shared his hellish nightmare.

Then, he told the poignant story of being released from a New York City jail, walking into Damascus Church on 162nd Street (then pastored by a husband-and-wife team, Francisco and Leoncia Rosado), and finding Jesus. Many immediately rose to their feet shouting and praising God. Others sat in amazement at the miracle God had done in John Gimenez' life.

As they sat down, John brought the message to a close. "What would you think if I told you everything I've just said couldn't be true?" he asked.

People were stunned. A few looked around, unsure of how to react to what they had just heard.

"In some peoples' books, that's the way it would be, because I got saved under a joint husband-wife pastoral ministry and some people can't accept that kind of ministry," he continued. "They believe a woman isn't supposed to be a minister. And if that's what you believe, you'll have to forget conversion stories like mine or else chalk them up as God's mistake."

With that, John walked off the platform past the pews where people sat in stunned silence. No one moved. He had left his audience—particularly the pastor—with a lot to consider.

෧෫෨

As we drove back to Coudersport, I wondered how many more such challenges the future held. Only time would tell. I knew and believed one simple fact above all: God had called me to the ministry and had joined my life with that of John Gimenez.

On our first Wednesday night back in Coudersport, we were seated in church when Brother Minor walked back to us and began praying. His prayer suddenly turned into a prophecy.

I am sending you forth to a people you know not of, he declared. *There I shall make you a great blessing...and I shall bless you mightily.*

That prophecy guided us like a bright light when we had to make major decisions about our future. About this time, we received an unexpected invitation to pastor a church back in Texas.

Years before, I had spent some months pastoring a small church in Corpus Christi. Its current pastor, Odell Allen, was leaving, and he wanted to know if John and I were interested in coming back to Corpus Christi to take his place.

When I told John of the inquiry, he remarked, "We can't be headed to Corpus. Brother Minor's prophecy said we were going to a people we don't know...and you know those people in Texas."

"That's right," I agreed. "God must have something else in mind."

Throughout the spring and into early summer of 1968, we traveled and held meetings, with me doing most of the preaching. John frequently gave his testimony and showed the movie *Way Out,* which resulted in many decisions for the Lord.

One day, John remembered Pat Robertson's invitation to come to Virginia Beach and called him to inquire about an available time. They settled upon a July date for him to appear on *The 700 Club.*

When July came, we were naturally excited about this opportunity to appear on television. John gave his testimony and together we sang Scripture choruses.

Chapter 9: Women Preachers

The audience's reception was warm and enthusiastic, especially when we sang "The Devil's Mad and I'm Glad." My use of a tambourine apparently inspired many viewers to go out and purchase one. Most Tidewater music stores, including the stamp redemption centers, quickly exhausted their supplies of tambourines after the show aired.

Before we left the Tidewater area, John had an unusual dream. "You won't believe it," he remarked over breakfast one morning.

"Well, tell me," I responded.

He took a sip of coffee. "I dreamed I went to the mailbox and got out a big white envelope. When I opened it, there were two tickets to Bogotá in there."

"Ohhh," I groaned. "I'm not all that interested in making a return trip to South America yet."

But that night, as we watched *The 700 Club* in our motel room, we heard Pat Robertson announce: "I'm planning a return trip to Bogotá, Colombia. We'll be ministering in several places and completing arrangements for the purchase of a Christian radio station."

"Wow," John enthused, clapping his hands. "Isn't that something?"

Immediately he picked up the phone, called *The 700 Club* and left a message for Pat. "Tell him that I had a dream about getting two tickets for Bogotá in the mail," he announced. "I don't know how it's going to happen, but I believe God wants us to go with this group in October."

When Pat got the message, he relayed it over the air with a broad grin. Days later—to everybody's surprise but John's—an acquaintance handed him the exact money we needed to purchase the roundtrip tickets to Bogotá.

❧❧

We spent the month of August in meetings around Detroit, where we celebrated our first wedding anniversary before traveling back to Coudersport. In early September, we returned to Tidewater, where we had a busy month of speaking engagements, a book signing event for John's new book, and another appearance on *The 700 Club*.

CBN also arranged several places for us to minister, including one popular charismatic church in Newport News. We were scheduled to preach a three-day series of meetings there, and John had planned for me to minister on the second night.

The church, however, had other ideas, as we soon learned. That night, a young man from the church arrived to drive us to the service. As we rode along, he remarked, "Brother John, the pastor wanted me to remind you of our doctrinal position on women in the church."

"What's that?" John asked.

"We hold to the words of 1 Corinthians 14:34-35 which says that a woman should keep silent in the church," he responded.

"Ahh, I see," John acknowledged, drawing a deep breath. He shot a look at me, seated comfortably in the back seat. I just shrugged my shoulders.

That night as we walked into the church, I noticed the pastoral team and the elders seated on the front row. "Good evening, Brother Gimenez," was their greeting as they moved over to give him room to sit down. Only one extra person could sit in the space they provided, and apparently it was going to be John.

I stood still momentarily, waiting to see if they'd also make room for me. When they didn't, I walked back to another aisle and took a seat. *I must be invisible*, I thought to myself.

All three nights I received the same treatment. Nobody acted as if I were present. The last night before we left, the pastor followed us out to the parking lot and greeted me for the first time. "Thanks for being with us, Sister Anne," he said cheerfully.

"Oh, you're welcome," I replied, smiling back at him.

But as we drove away, I expressed my frustration at how these leaders had conducted themselves toward me. "I've had rank sinners treat me with more kindness than these people," I said to John.

"I know, honey," he replied, reaching over to take my hand. "I think these people were just threatened by you...and when people are threatened, they act real peculiar."

This church's opposition to women in ministry truly surprised me. For over four years, God had opened doors for me to preach, and I had done so. I had traveled extensively as a single woman evangelist, and had been graciously accepted by the churches where I ministered. Frequently, I was invited back. I had also preached at large camp meetings all over the country and in Canada.

But apparently, I would continue to encounter churches that were unwilling to let women use the gifts God gave them for ministry. I decided I had better get used to such opposition. It wasn't going to disappear any time soon.

Born to Preach

Chapter 10

An Empty Building

Lens Avenue first rented building

Born to Preach

Chapter 10

An Empty Building

"I know where there's an empty church building available. Would y'all be interested in seeing it?"

—*Question asked of John & Anne, October 1968.*

John and I stayed several days at the house of a friend of CBN, Dorothy Baxter, upon our return to the Tidewater area. One day, when Dorothy and I were alone, she remarked to me, "I really wish you folks would stay in this vicinity and start a church."

I did not respond to Dorothy's suggestion, but inside I wondered, "Start a church? That's so strange for her to suggest that. She doesn't even know us. I've never preached here and John has only given his testimony. Why would she say such a thing?"

That night before going to bed, I told John what Dorothy had said. "God showed me we'll know where to stop and where to plant ourselves," he said simply, "because there'll be an empty church building."

"You think there's an empty church building just sitting around waiting for you?" I asked.

"Honey, I know God spoke to my heart," he replied softly.

Several nights later we drove from Denbigh, where we were staying with Dorothy, across the James River Bridge and on into Portsmouth to appear on *The 700 Club*. As we walked into CBN's main lobby, a smiling woman approached me with an outstretched hand. Her first words to me were, "My name's Betty Forbes, and I know where there's an empty church building..."

Her statement came from "out of the blue." Remembering John's words of the previous night, I pointed to where he stood and stuttered, "T-T-Tell him."

Still smiling warmly, the woman repeated herself to John. "I know where there's an empty church building. Would y'all be interested in seeing it?"

"You bet!" he exclaimed heartily. "When can we go?"

"I'll find out and call you," Betty graciously promised.

Arrangements were hastily made to see the building Saturday afternoon. As it turned out, Betty couldn't drive us, so she sent her best friend and fellow Methodist, Hazel Sasser. "I've tried but haven't been able to get in touch with anybody about getting into the building." Hazel explained, "So I don't have a key. But we can still look the place over if that's okay with you."

The church building turned out to be a well-kept, white frame structure at the corner of Lens Avenue and Kitchener Avenue in Norfolk. I had seen hundreds of similar buildings during my travels. But this church had an interesting history in the Pentecostal Holiness denomination since it found its roots directly from the Azusa Street Revival.

Betty's mother, Mayme Farr, lived on a street directly behind the church, and Betty told her that Hazel would be bringing us to look at the building. As we climbed out of the car, Mrs. Farr came around the corner. "Can another soul join the party?" she called out cheerfully.

"Sure, come on," John laughed.

After we finished inspecting the property, John suggested, "Why don't we pray and just commit this to the Lord?"

The four of us linked hands, and John and I raised our voices in unison to God. "Oh, God, whatever You want. If this is where You want us, Lord, we're willing…just make us to know, God… we praise You and thank You for the answer."

Hazel and Mrs. Farr looked a little uneasy when we finished praying. It was obvious they were not accustomed to the kind of fervent praying that John and I often did.

"We're leaving for Bogotá in the morning," John explained to Hazel. "But we'll be back the following Saturday night. Is there any chance of getting a key to this place?" She graciously promised to look into the situation for us.

We spent the next week in Bogotá, Colombia. Upon returning to the States, we were anxious to hear what Hazel had found out and called her almost immediately. The news was good: a key would be available Sunday afternoon.

Sure enough, an Assemblies of God minister identified only as Brother Mason came at the appointed time and showed us through the building. Hazel, Betty and several of their friends came along to pray.

A short, friendly man, Brother Mason explained that the church had been pastored by a husband-wife team from the

Pentecostal Holiness church. They had recently built a larger building and sold the Lens Avenue structure to the Assemblies of God.

"Our efforts at planting a church here did not work out," he concluded, "and so our denomination has put the building up for sale."

John and I both noticed the building was fully equipped to hold services immediately. Songbooks and offering plates stood neatly in place in the pews. Tables and chairs decorated the Sunday School rooms. A baptismal pool and public address system completed the sanctuary. A pastor's office was housed in the rear. The only thing lacking was a pastor and a congregation.

Someone suggested that we pray over the building. A message in tongues soon came forth and Brother Mason interpreted.

"The Lord has this day set before you an opened door," he declared, "and you should step through in lively faith believing in His Name…trust Him…believe Him…obey Him."

We were impressed with the facilities and especially touched by the prophetic word. Yet a problem materialized immediately over use of the building. Brother Mason made it clear the Assemblies of God wanted to *sell* the building.

"Is there any possibility your board would rent us the building until we see if a congregation can develop here?" John asked.

Brother Mason thought for a moment. "Tell you what," he said kindly. "Call me back tonight and I'll try to find out if the board will consider renting it."

That night following church, John called Brother Mason and learned that he had hit a proverbial "brick wall." The answer was no. The board members told him they couldn't possibly consider the matter until their official meeting in three weeks.

John was discouraged. "Let's go get our clothes packed," he said glumly. "We're going to Atlanta tomorrow."

❧

I didn't understand Brother Mason's answer to John, and I wasn't going to let the matter rest until I'd spoken with him myself. I called him back and asked innocently, "Can you explain this to me?"

Patiently, he described the situation to me. "Sister, the full board of the church has to vote on this matter. We can't even call a board meeting for three weeks. That's a requirement for churches and non-profit organizations in the State of Virginia and I can't change that.

"In the past, others have asked to rent the building and the board has always voted no," he continued. "And frankly, there's not much reason to expect them to change their minds and vote 'yes' now."

"Well then, would you consider renting the building for the next three weeks for us to have an evangelistic meeting?" I asked cheerfully. "We'll clean it up. It would be safe from vandals, and we'll take full responsibility. It's sitting empty right now."

"Well..." he started to say.

"Just consider renting us the building," I said sweetly, "while you're waiting on your board to decide if you can rent it."

"I tell you what," he offered kindly. "I'll have to call everybody on the board and it'll be tomorrow before I can do that.

Why don't you or your husband call me back tomorrow night. I'll try to have an answer by then."

My suggestion, I knew, would sound illogical to the board. Why would they rent a building for three weeks, and then have a meeting to decide if they would rent it? But on the other hand, God might just use my proposal for His purposes. At least that's the way I explained it to John.

We didn't leave for Atlanta the next day, and John called Brother Mason shortly after nine that night. "I don't understand it," he said, sounding puzzled. "But the board has agreed to rent the building until they can have a business meeting to decide whether or not to rent it. You can come over and pick up the key."

"Wonderful," John shouted.

Within a matter of days, we had electrical power reconnected to the building (which was a miracle itself) and one night some thirty people came to clean the place. Everybody sang praises while sweeping floors, cleaning windows, and dusting pews.

Then, we placed a tiny ad in *The Virginian-Pilot* newspaper. It simply read: "Revival meeting with John and Anne Gimenez, 3101 Lens Avenue, beginning October 20th."

A "camp meeting" style revival followed during the next two weeks. God moved sovereignly to save and heal people, and many were filled with the Holy Spirit. Spirit-filled believers—like Hazel Sasser and Betty Forbes—from the nearby Fairmount Park Methodist Church brought their friends from near and far.

❧

By the end of the second week, we were convinced God's hand lay upon this venture of faith. Still, we hadn't heard anything from Brother Mason about our continued use of the building.

One afternoon I called my mother with news of God's blessings in Virginia. "And we've found this beautiful little church that'll seat 250," I told her. "It's tailor-made for what we need. The only problem is the people who own it want to sell."

"Don't buy it," mother said flatly.

"Why not?" I questioned, startled at my mother's boldness.

"God just makes me know in my heart that this building isn't big enough for what He's going to do with you and John in that area," she replied confidently.

The conversation eventually lapsed into small talk about family and friends. But afterwards, I couldn't get away from Mother's words. *Where could my own mother come up with words like that? I pondered. I'd not heard her speak that way before. Could it be God?*

Brother Mason called one night asking if we could meet for coffee the next morning. "We've heard that God is moving beautifully in the little building," he said when we sat down at the diner. "The blessing of God is evidently upon what you folks are doing."

"I don't think we've had a night without people being saved and filled with the Holy Spirit," John said. "We are so grateful."

"It's been wonderful," I agreed.

Brother Mason paused for a moment, took a sip of coffee, and cleared his throat. "Well, we've had our meeting," he said with a grin, "and the board has decided to rent you the building."

"Oh, hallelujah!" John and I chorused, hugging one another, and then reaching to shake Brother Mason's hand.

"This is beautiful," John beamed.

"But," Brother Mason continued, gesturing expressively with his hands, "the building is *still* for sale and we'll make every effort to sell it—including placing a 'for sale' sign on the lawn."

I glanced at John and smiled. "That's no problem," he responded. "God's led us this far. He's put us here and we'll just have to trust Him to take care of the building situation."

It seemed to us that provision of the building was like a signpost guiding our steps saying: "…this is the way…" (Isaiah 30:21).

❧

During this time, I didn't tell John, but I had been trying to get pregnant for about six months. I was already thirty-six and knew the clock was ticking, and above all, I wanted a baby.

Silently, I had been praying that if we were to stay in Virginia Beach, God would allow me to conceive. A month after we began holding services, I scheduled an appointment with the doctor to confirm what I suspected—that I was pregnant. Unknown to me, John too, had been praying for a similar confirmation that we were to remain in the Tidewater area.

Then, the Sunday before my appointment, I started to miscarry. At the hospital, I was told I was losing tissue, and a dilation and curettage procedure (DNC) needed to be performed.

I couldn't believe what was happening. I had believed the promise of a child was confirmation to stay in Tidewater. Now, I was losing that child.

Chapter 10: An Empty Building

Yet, the whole time I was in the hospital the words of Psalm 119:11 continued to run through my mind and thoughts. *"Thy Word have I hid in mine heart, that I might not sin against thee"* (KJV).

Although we were devastated by the loss, I continued to hold onto what I believed was the promise of a child. Friends and family expressed their concern primarily for me, but John was also greatly affected.

One night we were watching a movie about a family who had lost a child at birth. As the emotions of the baby's parents spilled out of the screen, John began to weep. Through his tears, he told me of his heartache over the loss of our child.

One day when I called Brother Minor in Coudersport, his wife, Loraine, answered the phone.

"Well, Anne, I dreamed about you last night," she said happily. "I was ironing in my bedroom and looked up and you were standing in the doorway holding a little baby in your hands. The child had brown eyes and dark hair.

"In the dream I said, 'Anne Gimenez, whose baby is that?' You answered, 'She's mine and she's six months old.'"

Naturally, I was thrilled at Loraine's dream. In fact, I was pregnant at the time and didn't know it.

I preached up until my eighth month of pregnancy. But John, who had only ever shared his testimony, was forced to take over for me in the last month. He had always encouraged me to preach, but now that he was compelled to do so, his gifting to minister emerged beautifully.

When I discovered that I was pregnant, I knew I would be thrilled with either a boy or a girl. But I told my mother, "If I have a little girl, I will think that God dropped a part of Heaven in my heart!"

Later, a visiting preacher was staying with us while holding special services at the church. By then, my condition had become obvious.

"What are you going to name that little girl?" he asked one morning, walking into the kitchen.

"Oh, do you think that's what it'll be?" I asked smiling.

"Sure do," he said.

And he was right. Finally, our baby girl, Robin Anne Gimenez, was born very early in the morning of January 30, 1970. John had promised he would not leave the hospital until the baby arrived, but—pressured by a meeting already scheduled in Newport News—he went and preached. When he returned, I was still in labor. He heard someone screaming in the nearby delivery room and thought, *That's not Anne.* But it was!

❧

When I first saw Robin, she was tiny and pink. She also had brown eyes and dark hair, just like the child in Loraine Minor's dream.

Several months before Robin's birth, John had announced one night that the church would be named "Rock Church."

"And the gates of hell will not prevail against it," he declared. "This will be the foundation stone upon which many lives will be built… I know it will happen."

The only church we'd ever known with that name was in midtown Manhattan, where I had preached several times. But John

Chapter 10: An Empty Building

felt "Rock Church" was what God wanted us to name the congregation. And so we did.

People from all over Tidewater continued to jam into the white frame building at 3101 Lens Avenue in Norfolk. It had been constructed to hold 250 people comfortably, but now 350 crowded into the little church every Sunday. The Sunday School rooms were full, and people stood in lines outside waiting until the doors opened.

One Sunday morning, the Lord gave me a vision as I stood on the platform. I saw a hand pull a window shade down and release it. The shade rolled all the way to the top. Bright sunlight streamed through the window, and I heard the Lord speak: *The stigma over the baptism of the Holy Spirit will be lifted and rolled back. Light will come flooding in.*

Within a matter of days, a series of articles on the Jesus Movement captured the pages of *Life* magazine and the interest of the nation. Rock Church was flooded with new people—more than seventy-five percent of them under age twenty-five. The Jesus Movement had hit Tidewater.

Our congregation began to grow as we reached out to the community. John would share his testimony in clubs and at high school assemblies, speaking of the horrors he had gone through as an addict. Although he couldn't talk about Jesus, he could give his testimony

John would say, "The only cured addict is a dead addict." Often people would ask, " Well, then how come you're off of it?" John would launch into his story of finding a church in the Bronx and how he gave himself to God. The Lord had rescued him, and given his life hope and meaning.

Young people began coming to the church in increasing numbers. Their parents would follow as they witnessed changes in their children's attitude and behavior. Gang members, students, mothers and fathers, and businessmen—people from every arena of life came and were saved and filled with the Holy Spirit.

The crowds at Rock Church soon grew so large that the building became something of a fire hazard. Without question, we would soon have to find larger facilities.

೧೨

After months of fruitless looking at other properties and listening to the opinions of a great variety of people, we took some time off in April 1970 to attend a church convention in Toronto. On our way home, we stopped off at Elim Bible Institute.

Elim's missions secretary, Costa Dier, was a small, balding man with a distinctive mustache which seemed to match his ebullient personality. He was his usual laughing, jovial self when we stepped into his office that day. He had kisses and hugs for both of us and for Robin, whom he was meeting for the first time. We shared with him about God's mighty blessings in the Tidewater area.

"That's beautiful what God is doing," Costa said warmly.

"But we need some answers, brother," John said seriously. "The main reason we took this trip was to hear from God. We've been seeking Him as to what our next step should be. We're actually thinking about buying and renovating an old building, but we're just not sure…"

Chapter 10: An Empty Building

Costa's eyes lit up. He stood up and exclaimed, "Folks, let's pray!"

We linked hands and everyone prayed fervently in the Spirit for some time. Then, the word of the Lord came to Costa.

Arise and build, he proclaimed, *for I have called thee to build a tabernacle unto Me. Build for the thousands...arise and build... arise and build.*

"I wish that I could be with you, because there's going to be a spiritual explosion in the Tidewater area," he predicted. "That's why you're to build for the thousands. Get ready...you really haven't seen anything yet."

Returning home, we announced to the church that God had given us fresh direction for the days ahead. We then shared Costa's prophecy that we were to "arise and build."

Upon hearing this, the congregation stood to their feet and began to shout, clap their hands, and worship the Lord. Most were under twenty-five wearing bib-overalls and sandals, and many had come to the Lord out of the drug culture.

Even though we had no property and no architectural plans for a building, we ventured out in faith—simply at the Word of the Lord. Obeying the voice of the Lord had always been a principle in our personal lives; now it would become a principle for Rock Church as well.

❦

In due time, a realtor in the church contacted us about five and a half acres of property located on Kempsville Road. "This is the very center of Tidewater right here," he explained, "and this is where the building corridor is going. Thousands of homes will be built here."

When John saw the property and the deep drainage ditches alongside Kempsville Road for the first time, he was dismayed. "That place is a dumping ground and full of snakes," he announced glumly.

In other ways, however, the property seemed ideal for us. Its most important attribute was—"location, location, location!"

As soon as contracts were signed for the property, we applied for a use permit from the Virginia Beach Planning Commission. Problems arose immediately. Rumors circulated that we intended to use the site for a drug rehab center. Petitions to keep Rock Church out of the Kempsville Road site were signed and neighborhood meetings were called to mobilize opposition. The protest grew continually louder.

We held our breath for several weeks as the Planning Commission gave Rock Church a top-to-bottom examination. Their final report was a bombshell; it recommended severe restrictions be added to the use permit.

If we wanted the use permit, we had to accept the restrictions so, reluctantly, John agreed to them. Next, the permit went before the entire city council, where more opposition loomed. The council meeting was tense, and it appeared our permit was doomed; then, unexpectedly, an Episcopal priest stood up in defense of our church.

"Those limitations you've placed on Rock Church are illegal in my view," he announced. "I don't believe you can put limitations on a church as to how it will operate, or whether it can bus people to its services. That's a violation of their constitutional rights."

In the end, the council struck down all limitations and voted to approve the permit 10-1. At last, after months of opposition, Rock Church could go forward and build on its land.

The victory was sweet, but valuable time had been lost in the struggle. More than three months had passed from the time the contract was signed until a spade broke the ground. John and I knew that the battle had only been won through the prayer and fasting of God's people.

We paid $5,000 down on the land and financed the balance. John then went to a bank asking for a $100,000 loan to build the sanctuary. Almost 400 people were attending Rock Church at the time, and we thought the congregation's size would ensure that there would be no problem securing a loan.

When the banker questioned John about his background, he did not hold back. He shared the details of his past, including his conversion to Christ. Unfortunately, the banker was not impressed, and we did not get the loan.

In spite of this setback, we had a word from heaven that said, "Build," and we went forward with the plan to build. Our architect's plans called for a 450-seat auditorium, six classrooms, a nursery, a prayer room, and a fellowship hall.

One day, John came home and announced, "Winter's coming and we've got to get cement in the ground." Within a few days, he had gotten some men together and dug footings for the new building.

Shortly afterwards, I received a call from the lawyer of the people who were selling us the property. "Mrs. Gimenez, my clients would like to know what you're doing on their property?" he asked.

"Winter's coming," I answered, "and we need to get cement in the ground."

"That's fine," he replied, "but we need to have a *proper* closing before you do anything else out there."

We had yet to complete that final step in buying the land. For John, having a word from heaven had been enough; he simply then went out, got a shovel, and said, "Let's build!"

Soon after, we officially closed on the property, paying all the legal fees, and also paid $10,000 for the concrete slab for the building. By then, the church coffers were empty. We didn't have a dime left for a single brick.

John, however, forged ahead with the building effort just as if the church had a bank account bulging with money. Except for highly specialized sub-contracting jobs, church members did all the construction work. John donned a tattered pair of jeans and began digging ditches.

On the first of each month, he brought the bills before the church. "Here they are," he would announce. "Let's praise the Lord for His goodness and His supply."

God's supply never failed. It always equaled Rock Church's need. Everyone soon learned that, when God gave His Word on a matter, it would be done. Anticipation arose in the hearts of the people as to what mighty deeds God might accomplish in the future.

Dedication day came on May 22, 1971. Some eight hundred people showed up for the opening services, overflowing the main sanctuary and requiring extra seats to be set up. David Minor came down from Coudersport to preach that day. He reacted like a proud father, rejoicing at what God was doing in our midst.

The Lord had said *Build,* and we had obeyed.

When the church doors opened for the first service, everything was paid for, including construction materials and labor, right down to the pews, carpets, chairs, and piano. The church was debt-free. It was a great time of celebration for us.

The joyous, praise-filled services that had characterized our meetings on Lens Avenue continued in high gear when we moved into the facility on Kempsville Road. In fact, the spontaneity and freedom of worship hit a new level. We all learned moving to a new, unfamiliar location in no way prevented people from entering into new realms of worship; the crucial issue was to obey God. The anointing of the Lord always follows such obedience.

Each Sunday, more people flocked to our new location on Kempsville Road. Within a month or so following the dedication, the sanctuary was overflowing. Freshly built walls then had to be ripped out from the sides and back of the sanctuary so the space could be used to accommodate the crowds. Next, the six classrooms, social hall and nursery were eliminated. Still, it wasn't enough; more space was soon needed.

After nine months in the new building, nearly all of the original interior walls had been ripped out so we could expand the auditorium. Even that wasn't enough. With 1,400 people now attending, we had to begin holding two morning services.

❧❧❧

The Jesus Movement was in full swing; the community was hungry and receptive. People came in such overwhelming numbers that at times, even with two services, not everyone could get in the doors. Some of them then went next door to the Presbyterian Church, growing their congregation.

John and I were stunned at the growth. We honestly weren't sure what to do next to accommodate the crowds. Then, one of the construction crew made a suggestion. He could put a balcony in without much trouble.

"You're right," John said. "There's no place else to expand right now. What do you need?"

"Just buy the material," the man offered, "and I'll build it."

"It's a deal," John agreed.

The balcony took shape rapidly, but even that extra space didn't suffice for long. It was astounding. The church had been designed to seat 450 people, and it had filled up the very first Sunday. In a few short months, attendance had jumped to a thousand people at each service, and more new faces appeared each week.

As the church's growth continued unabated, John got distracted by another project dear to his heart—helping the troubled, drug-using young people he continually encountered.

He had found an old hunting lodge—a rambling wooden structure sitting on five acres in Backbay, near the North Carolina/Virginia border—that reminded him of "Mountaindale," the retreat in upstate New York where he and several of the Addicts had gone after their conversions.

Chapter 10: An Empty Building

John had hoped someday to duplicate that ministry and now was dreaming of converting the lodge he had found into a drug rehabilitation house. He forged ahead, negotiating a price for the hunting lodge and raising a $5,000 down payment. Then, obstacles cropped up, and voices of opposition challenged the use permit before the local Planning Commission.

Dealing with these problems occupied much of John's time and attention, and kept him from focusing on the immediate need for more space for our church structure. We needed God's direction for this problem.

One Sunday as we were leaving the church, I had a vision of a long, two-story building extending out from the back of our present sanctuary. I could hardly wait to tell John what I had just seen.

"Oh, John," I enthused. "I know what we're going to do next."

"What do you mean *next*?" he asked, as he wheeled the car out of the church parking lot and onto Kempsville Road.

"I just saw a long, two-story building in a vision," I explained. "It'll be the educational building and we'll construct it directly from the back of the main building."

"Hmmmm," he mumbled, obviously not particularly interested in what I'd seen. I realized then that John simply wasn't in a place where he could hear my words. His focus was on the halfway house project in Backbay. But I was sure that, in God's timing, he would hear me.

The following Tuesday night, I told the congregation about the vision. "I don't know if it was an experience like Daniel had or not," I confessed, "but I know what I saw—just as plain as day."

Instead of groaning at the prospect of more construction, the crowd exploded with applause. They stood up, shouting, singing, and praising God.

Soon afterwards, a building contractor told me he would donate all electrical work for the new building, including installation and supplies.

The church leadership quickly met to discuss the building and parking situation, and they agreed to move ahead. When the new addition ended up exactly in the spot where I'd seen it in my vision, John admitted quietly, "You were right all the time."

I laughed and, resisting the urge to say, "I told you so," added simply, "I know what I saw."

Nine months later, the new educational wing was completed. Just like the sanctuary, it was built by the men of the church and was debt free when finished. Over $170,000 had been donated to pay for the construction costs.

At the same time, the Backbay project was resolved. After weeks of opposition and conflict, John received a prophetic word that he would *no longer be involved in rehabilitation but in discipleship training...* At first, he was reluctant to accept the prophecy. Yet, inwardly, he felt God had spoken and, in obedience, he withdrew his plans.

It was good when John once again gave his full attention to the church, so that we had a single focus. We were continually astounded at God's unfolding favor and blessing upon the church. At times, we wondered if there could possibly be more.

Chapter 11
A Round Church

*Pastor Anne in the
round sanctuary, 1975*

Born to Preach

Chapter 11

A Round Church

"Arise and build for I have called thee to build a tabernacle unto Me. Build for the thousands...arise and build...arise and build."

—*prophecy from Costa Dier*

Within two years, Rock Church had outgrown every inch of available space. For over a year, we had held two morning services to accommodate the growing numbers of people. It was time to build again and just about everybody knew it.

One day, I was in John's office talking with him about a matter when he abruptly said, "I know what we're going to do next."

"What?" I asked.

"We'll put up another building, and I just feel in my heart that the building's gonna be round," he said.

Yet, neither of us had a clear word of direction from the Lord—and that's what we had always operated on. We felt that Costa Dier's prophecy to "build for the thousands" was yet to be fulfilled. So, we waited for confirmation.

One muggy afternoon, John was driving down Kempsville Road toward the church, intending to do an errand in Tidewater. When he reached the property, however, the Holy Spirit told him to "walk off" the new church building. As he drove onto the church grounds, the Spirit came upon him and he began speaking in tongues.

Getting out of the car, John began walking rapidly around the utility pole that was in the center of our five acres. He was speaking in tongues with his hands raised and his knees going up and down like pistons in an engine. For several minutes, he walked in a circle around the light pole.

Cars were whizzing past on Kempsville Road, but John continued circling the pole. Finally, he stopped and headed towards the building. Only then did he notice the bus that had pulled into the parking lot bringing visitors to the church. Several of them smiled broadly as John walked past. They had evidently witnessed his strange antics in the parking lot.

"From that experience," he told me, "I know God wants us to build a round building. I have no doubt of that." I agreed, and we moved forward.

The following Sunday, John and I described to the church the direction God was leading in the project, and a "token" building fund offering of $30,000 was received. "Somebody go get a shovel," John said, grinning with obvious delight.

John and I and the entire congregation—more than a thousand people in all—promptly marched out the door and, using the shovel, broke ground. The new round building was underway.

Chapter 11: A Round Church

The usual problems cropped up immediately—construction permits, regulations with the city, and, of course, paying the bills.

As had been done with the first sanctuary, Rock Church paid cash as the new building took shape. John presented the construction bills each week and received an offering. The collection always covered the bills.

Usually, the bills totaled between $20,000 and $30,000. But one particular Sunday, we needed over $100,000 *by the very next morning*. The contractor would proceed no further without that amount being paid.

That morning, John stood and spoke to the congregation. "Folks, I've prayed, and I feel God told me a hundred men would stand with me this morning and give a thousand dollars apiece. As the church's pastors, Anne and I are giving the first thousand."

With hands raised, we began worshiping and praising the Lord. The band fell in behind us. The choir sang and the sounds of worship filled the sanctuary.

Slowly, people began coming down the aisles and leaving their checks at the altar. Those who came first remained in the front of the church as more came forward. When the altar call stopped, more than a hundred were standing there.

I knew it would take a miracle from God for some of them to come up with that kind of money in a day or so. Yet, the money came. Construction never lagged. No one person would ever be able to take credit for the building, not John or me. Only a sovereign move of God could have made this possible.

Dedication day came in May 1977—seven years after Costa Dier's prophecy exhorting us *to arise and build for the thousands*.

The thousands were here now, and they had donated more than two million dollars for the new sanctuary.

As the congregation took possession of the new building, only $100,000 was owed. That debt was paid in a few weeks, leaving the 2,500-seat building debt free. Praise God!

It was a great feeling to complete the building project and to have everything paid for. Little did I know that in the years to come, we would eventually build again to accommodate even more worshipers.

୰ৡৡ

Later that same summer when John was out of town, I attended the dedication of a new Assemblies of God church in Tidewater. Pat Robertson was the guest speaker. After the ceremony, I approached him and invited him for a Sunday night service at Rock Church. He agreed to come.

The night Pat came, the building was packed with the largest crowd to date in the new sanctuary. During the service, he reminisced about the days when God first sent him to Tidewater. "It was a spiritual wasteland then," he said, "but God told me it would become a watering place."

Later that night, we went to dinner with Pat and talked about going back on television. We'd previously telecast our church services, but due to our building program, we'd been off the air for about two years. "Is there any chance of getting our television program on CBN?" John asked.

"If you can give us a quality program, you can be on satellite all over the country," Pat answered. "You'll reach about 15 million people or more."

Chapter 11: A Round Church

He promised to put us in touch with some of CBN's broadcast pros. We learned quickly that the new round shape of our building was almost perfect for doing a television program.

On the first anniversary of the new building's dedication—May 1978—our new TV program hit the airwaves. Response was immediate. "When I see your program, I feel like I've been to church," one man wrote.

"I used to go to a church like yours," a letter acknowledged. "I didn't know there were any churches around like that today."

There were other, less complimentary letters, too. Some complained about "women preachers"; others objected to the 27-piece orchestra. But such letters were by far in the minority of those we received.

In time, we came to see the great blessing of televising services. In a single telecast, we could reach more people than we had in years of preaching. Certain well-meaning counselors who in previous years had advised us to stay in evangelism instead of pastoring would have been astounded to see us ministering to tens of thousands by way of television.

Born to Preach

Chapter 12
Washington for Jesus

Washington for Jesus, 1980

Born to Preach

Chapter 12

Washington for Jesus

"If My people which are called by My name will humble themselves, and pray, and seek My face, and turn from their wicked ways, then will I hear from heaven, and will forgive their sin, and will heal their land."

—*2 Chronicles 7:14 (NKJV)*

It was during a conference in Oakland, California, in October 1978 that John received the vision for Washington for Jesus. This historic march in our nation's capital ultimately affected the lives of hundreds of thousands and may have influenced the presidential election of 1980, sending Ronald Reagan to the White House.

As John was preaching that day, God began speaking to him about bringing His people together. He read from 1 Samuel 17, the story of David and Goliath—specifically verse 29, where David asked the question, "Is there not a cause?"

God began to show John that there was a cause and a message. Even as there was a Goliath in the time of David, John preached, there was another Goliath today seeking to destroy the American system that has always been based on the Word of God.

John and I, as well as the organizers of Washington for Jesus, began to believe that perhaps one million Christians would come to Washington, D.C., on April 29, 1980, to demonstrate to the nation and the world that the Church of Jesus Christ meant business with God.

That specific date—April 29th—had been chosen because of its historical significance. It was the anniversary of the 1607 planting of the cross by Robert Hunt, chaplain of the Jamestown colony, in dedication of America's first settlement. John felt that we were to pray on that date when centuries before, America was dedicated to God in prayer and the land was committed to the proclamation of the Gospel of Jesus Christ.

For more than two years, John traveled continuously from one side of America to the other gathering support and building interest in Washington for Jesus. Pat Robertson of CBN and Bill Bright of Campus Crusade for Christ were chosen as program co-chairmen, with John serving as the national chairman.

In preparation for the day of the march, we held a Christian women's leadership rally at Constitution Hall with some four thousand attending. I spoke to the gathering along with Dede Robertson, Vonette Bright, Dale Evans Rogers, Shirley Boone, Dee Jepsen and Sarah Jordan Powell.

The next night, a pastor's conference was held in the same location with leaders such as Dr. James Kennedy, James Robison, David du Plessis, and the magnificent preacher, Bishop Jesse Winley.

Chapter 12: Washington for Jesus

That same night, some 30,000 young people gathered in the rain at RFK Stadium for a youth rally and to hear Evangelist Arthur Blessitt and the legendary Keith Green. Many remained to pray till early morning in final preparation for the march.

The rally was scheduled to take place between 6 a.m. and 6 p.m. the next day. For nearly three days, Washington's weather had featured nothing but a continual downpour, and the forecast was not encouraging. We all wondered if the weather would affect the turnout.

John and I were staying in a hotel near the Smithsonian. On the morning of April 29th, we awoke in the pre-dawn darkness. As we dressed, John looked at me and said, "Anne, I don't know if anybody will be there but us."

I guess my prophetic nature kicked in. "John, it doesn't matter," I replied. "God sent us and we're here. Let's go."

We went down to the lobby, where several of the speakers were already gathered, and headed out. There was a damp mist in the air and the sky was gray and overcast. The weather was anything but inviting.

Yet, by the time we arrived at the Mall, people were coming from seemingly every direction. Many arrived by train, getting off the Metro and joining the ever-swelling crowd on the Mall.

By mid-morning, the entire 23-block-long Mall between the Washington Monument and the Capitol Building was teeming with people. Many were calling it the largest religious gathering in the history of the United States. By mid-afternoon, the National Park Service estimated the crowd to be over 700,000 "and still growing."

Dark clouds still covered the sky when Pastor E.V. Hill from Mt. Zion Missionary Baptist Church in Los Angeles stood up to pray about 10 a.m. The prayer was a simple and heartfelt confession to God.

"We come here today not seeking power from the government, but we're asking that Thy Holy Spirit, which is *the* power, will fall upon us afresh and anew. We believe You're going to save us from the wrath that is sure to come unless we repent.

"We acknowledge our weaknesses and our wickedness. We acknowledge that we have strayed far from Thee. But we know that Thou art a loving God…Thou art a tender God…Thou art a merciful God and so we say, in the Name of Jesus, save us Lord… restore us Lord…bless us Lord."

As Dr. Hill prayed in his deep resonate voice, the threatening storm clouds parted and the warm sun suddenly shone down brilliantly. Thousands cheered and shouted praises to God. That opening of bright sun and blue sky was surely a token of God's love and grace.

We had a state-by-state parade of people on the Capitol Mall—thousands marching with American flags and colorful banners. Those who had worn raincoats soon took them off, and many were fanning themselves in the humid air.

Leaders from every background and denomination were on hand to speak throughout the afternoon. Some preachers came from denominations that, under normal circumstances, could hardly speak to others. But *that* day, they locked arms and prayed together.

By six o'clock, when the event ended, not a drop of rain had fallen and marred the march.

Chapter 12: Washington for Jesus

ويص

Afterwards, John, Robin, our coordinator, Ted Pantaleo, and I walked across the street to a little coffee shop. As we sat there chatting happily about the day's events, it began to rain. In another thirty minutes, it was pouring.

That night in our hotel room, we watched the eleven o'clock news. Nothing was mentioned about the hundreds of thousands of believers who had come together to pray at the Capitol. The networks did report, however, that twelve protestors had poured red ink on the steps at the Pentagon.

The weatherman then came on and reported that a Canadian air mass was moving in, bringing still more rain to Washington, D.C. He then observed, "Strangely, the only area not affected by the heavy rain today was the Mall, where a couple of thousand people were meeting to pray."

The man then looked directly into the camera and said, "I guess those people would say their God did that."

I jumped up, shouting, "Yes, our God did that!"

Even though the National Park Service had estimated attendance at well past half a million "and growing", the only news coverage of the March that we ever saw was in the weather report.

Interestingly, then-President Jimmy Carter was unavailable to speak to the gathering, either in person or by phone. Ronald Reagan telephoned, declaring "I am with you." A little over six months later, Reagan was elected president. A number of men and women of God have often looked back at that day and concluded the Washington for Jesus campaign was probably the turning point in Reagan's election.

In fact, when Ronald Reagan was inaugurated on January 20, 1981, Dr. Bill Bright, founder of Campus Crusade for Christ, told the new President: "Some of us believe you were actually elected on April 29th when over 700,000 Christians came to Washington and prayed for America."

Washington for Jesus turned out to be one of the largest recorded gatherings in the history of the nation, outside of the Bicentennial celebrations in 1976. Some have even linked and credited the birth of the modern Conservative political movement to the massive network created by the first Washington for Jesus rally.

In time, we came to see the phenomenal results of answered prayer on that historic day: the release of the American hostages in Iran, the economic recovery of our nation, and the renewed unity among Christians from different denominations and movements.

John came home from D.C. with a vision to hold America for Jesus rallies in stadiums throughout the country, as a continuation of what happened at Washington for Jesus. The flame had been lit, and the fire had been ignited. People all over the United States were gathering to answer the call to prayer.

Rock Church purchased an 18-wheeler, together with a stage and a special public address system for outdoor events. Soon, we were traveling around the country, holding rallies.

Chapter 12: Washington for Jesus

❧

One of these events took place in Miami, Florida, at the Orange Bowl stadium. The day before the giant rally, as we rested in our hotel room, John received a phone call.

From where I sat in the living room, I could hear him talking but couldn't understand what the conversation was about. When I walked back into the bedroom, John was laying flat on his back looking up at the ceiling. "We just lost everything we have," he announced quietly.

"What are you talking about?" I asked.

"That was the Securities & Exchange Commission on the phone," he explained. "Our investment with our friend's company is frozen. The government is saying the whole thing is a Ponzi scheme. They're just notifying us we're one of the victims…we've just lost all that we had."

We had recently sold our house and used some of the money to contribute to the purchase of the church's 18-wheeler. We had then invested the remainder—about $100,000—in what turned out to be a fraudulent enterprise.

I stood there a moment trying to take in what John had said. I could see that he was simply devastated by the loss of our "nest egg."

I was quiet for a few moments and then walked over to where he was lying on the bed. "So what?" I said matter-of-factly. "We still love each other and we love God. And tomorrow, we're going back from here to a church that loves us…so what?"

"You're right," he smiled. "So what?" We picked ourselves up, completed the meeting in Miami, and never looked back.

❧❧

The Washington for Jesus rally was a great success. However, we came home with over $200,000 in debts that our church had to pay. Some who had been part of the gathering, made financial commitments that they didn't honor, and we were left holding the bills. We resolved never to take our church into that kind of debt again.

Around seven years later, God began dealing with both John and me about the need to hold another Washington for Jesus event. We had gone to Washington the first time to call the nation to prayer. Now, the Church itself needed to repent. After a time of prayer, I agreed with John that we should go back and hold a Washington for Jesus 1988.

The second rally came right on the heels of some notable scandals among television preachers. Some religious leaders had suggested we'd never be able to get the "believers" to come together again as they had in 1980.

But Pat Robertson and Bill Bright—men of prayer and great influence—both agreed with us that the Church should return to Washington. "We believe God gave you this vision," they each told John, "and we'll follow you."

After both Pat and Bill signed on again, John wrote to the leaders of many major denominations, including Adrian Rogers of the Southern Baptist Convention and Ben Armstrong of the National Religious Broadcasters. They all agreed it was time to return to Washington.

Chapter 12: Washington for Jesus

To our amazement, the crowds in the spring of 1988 were even larger than in 1980—nearly one million people converged on the National Mall to pray!

Leaders such as Oral Roberts, Pat Robertson, Bill Bright, Kenneth Copeland, Morris Cerullo, James Dobson, Jack Hayford, Dr. E.V. Hill, James Robison, Demos Shakarian, Pat Boone, Wellington Boone, Corinthia Boone, Rosie Greer, Gigi Avila, and many others joined us in prayer for revival in the land.

The youth rally drew tens of thousands and featured multiple speakers, including a new musical group from Liberty University called "dc Talk". It was a powerful event that brought further unity to the Body of Christ. Yet, it would not be the last time God would call us to Washington to pray for America.

❧❧

In the fall of 1988, John went in for what we thought was routine gall bladder surgery. The surgeon called the operation a success and said that John would be fine. But day after day in the hospital, his condition showed no sign of improving. In fact, he seemed to grow weaker.

I knew something was wrong. In fact, I felt he was dying—in spite of everything his surgeon continued to say.

Several days passed. Finally, I called my secretary. "Please contact John's personal physician," I instructed. "He's not getting better, and I've got to get some treatment for him. He's too important to God, me, and everybody else for me to sit here and let him die."

When the doctor called, I explained the situation. "This surgeon says John is fine, but he's not recovering. I know in my heart he's dying and I've got to get him some help. I have to do something."

"If you hadn't asked for another doctor, I couldn't do anything," the physician told me, "but let me call you back."

Shortly afterwards, a specialist came in, examined John, and recommended several tests. When they were completed, he came back to the waiting room. "Mrs. Gimenez, we shot the dye in to locate the problem and it filled up his body cavity," he said. "Your husband obviously has a hole inside that we'll have to surgically repair."

Plans were made to stabilize John and then operate the following day. However, his vital signs started shutting down almost immediately, and he was rushed into surgery with Robin and me running behind the gurney, praying for him.

About ten o'clock that night, the specialist finally came out. "We found the problem," he said, "but your husband's not out of the woods yet."

Unknown to anyone, the sutures from the gall bladder surgery had ruptured, and peritonitis and pneumonia had set in. As one of the doctors said later, "Your husband came as close to dying as anybody could come without actually passing away."

The whole scenario occurred in October while Rock Church was holding its annual convention. For days, ministers who had come from all over the country to attend the convention filled the waiting room and offered unrelenting prayers for John.

We were never more grateful than when John recovered and was able to come home to us.

Chapter 13
Changing Times

Robin's wedding day, June 7, 1991

Born to Preach

Chapter 13

Changing Times

"The anointing is when you are separated from yourself and filled with God's glory so that when you speak, it's like God speaking and when you act, it's like God acting..."

—*Oral Roberts from a CBN interview with Michael Little, 2002.*

My father continued in television work in Corpus Christi until he faced mandatory retirement at age sixty-five. He and Mother then purchased a travel trailer and spent a number of years traveling the highways and byways of the country.

Then, one day in the mid-1980s, my father telephoned and announced, "We're going to move to Virginia Beach. I want your mother to be close to you in the event something ever happens to me."

For the next twenty years, my father put his media skills and experience to work in various departments of our ministry. Before moving to Virginia Beach, he had never actually gone to church. Now, he was in church whenever the doors were open.

Born to Preach

❦

Robin graduated from high school in 1988 and joined Youth with a Mission (YWAM). For about a year, she worked overseas, then came back home to work in our ministry. After returning, she met a tall, black-haired young man by the name of John Blanchard, who, after years of being an atheist, had just gotten saved.

John wanted to date Robin, but I put my foot down. I had a conversation with him one day. "I'm not going to force you to come to this church," I explained, "but my daughter isn't going to date anyone who doesn't."

He not only started coming to the church but went through our First Principles class for membership and became active in our prayer room, holding all-night prayer vigils with several other young men.

John and Robin spent most of their courting time together in our home, and after a year, approached us about marrying. After the engagement was official, John went to Dallas, Texas, and attended Christ for the Nations Institute for a semester. When he returned, they were married on June 7, 1991. Together, they completed another year of study at CFNI and continued to demonstrate a refreshing call of God upon their lives.

Our joy over Robin and John's marriage was made complete when they presented us with our first granddaughter, Amelia, on November 7, 1992.

Chapter 13: Changing Times

❦

During this time, John and I continued to co-pastor the church. Also, I traveled a great deal, speaking before groups like Women's Aglow in the States and overseas in Japan, Australia, the Philippines, and South Korea.

After the end of the Cold War in 1991, Bob Weiner, who led a ministry named Maranatha, invited a number of preachers from various organizations, including Rock Church, to preach rallies in both Russia and the Ukraine.

During the meetings in Kiev, my interpreter was Andre Yagin, a former officer in the Russian Army who had become a Christian. Later, we brought Andre to America for further training in ministry. When he returned to the Ukraine, he built homes for unwed mothers and pioneered several churches throughout the country and is a pastor in Sevastopol today.

I also started an organization, International Women in Leadership (IWILL), to specifically impact and encourage women in leadership positions. Evelyn Roberts, Gloria Copeland, Jane Hanson, and Dee Jepsen served on the board.

During one of the first board meetings, Evelyn Roberts cited the need for such an organization. "Ruth Graham and I were in similar positions at one time," she said. "Our husbands were very well known but we wives never got a chance to know each other. I just wish we had had something like this back then."

John and I came to know and love Oral Roberts, a man greatly used of God. John served on the Board of Regents of Oral Roberts University for a time, and we both received honorary doctorates from the school in 1985.

In the fifties, I had gone with a group from my church in Corpus Christi to one of Oral's great healing campaigns in San Antonio. I would have never dreamed then that one day I would know him and his wife personally, or that I would be honored by the school he founded. It would have simply been beyond my capacity to imagine such a thing happening to me.

⊷⊶

John Gimenez had an unusual, disarming manner about himself that was most effective in talking with others about their lives. He was particularly skillful in sharing the Gospel with those who were running from the call of God. One of the best examples of his success in that area is the impact he had upon Gordon Robertson.

In late 1993, John received a phone call from Pat Robertson saying he needed help for his youngest son, Gordon, whose problem with drug addiction had grown from experimental to severe. "I need you to do what you do best," Pat said.

About the same time, John had a dream about Gordon participating in a crusade in India. John called Gordon on the Thursday before the trip was to begin the following Monday. Gordon agreed to go, thinking that John could never obtain a visa in time for him to make the trip. To his great surprise, Gordon found himself in Rajamundry, India, the next week actively involved in the crusade.

What followed was a life-changing three-week episode for Gordon. John had him up speaking to crowds in the crusade, even though Gordon's own life was in shambles. Before the team was to return to the States, John had a second dream that Gordon remained in India.

Surprisingly, Gordon agreed with the dream and stayed behind after the team left. He subsequently had a "Damascus road experience," like the apostle Paul. He would later say, "Jesus has truly spoken to me."

Gordon was forever grateful for the role the self-effacing John Gimenez played in his life. But there were hundreds of others—most not as visible as Gordon—whose lives he touched in similar ways.

❦

In mid-1995, another Washington for Jesus rally was being planned for the next year, and I made a trip to Texas to raise support for the gathering. Mother was in her late 70s then, and I took her with me. Our first service was at Brother E.O. Allen's church, Southside Gospel Tabernacle in San Antonio, and we planned to head to Houston from there.

My mother's father was buried in San Antonio. She had been not quite seven years old when he died, and recently, she had expressed a desire to look for the gravesite. "I don't have any idea where the cemetery is now, but I'd like to visit my father's grave if we can find it," she told me several times.

Mother recalled that her father's gravestone was a Woodman of the World marker in the shape of a tree stump. With Brother Allen and his wife's help, we managed to find its location where we found the grave marker. It turned out to be exactly as Mother remembered.

As we stood gazing at the gravesite, thoughts of my grandfather flowed through my mind with a force that stunned me. For a moment, I thought I was going to faint. Everything that I'd ever heard about this man began filling my thoughts…all that Mother had spoken about her daddy…here he was…an actual person… and I was one of his descendants.

It was an extraordinary experience—one that I could never have anticipated. Mother seemed fine, talking about all the things she remembered about her father. But I was touched in the depths of my soul. To this day, I don't know why. I only know something deeply spiritual took place there.

I returned to Texas later that year because of the home-going of my Aunt Ruby, the woman who was truly my spiritual mother. She was the one who had once tenderly placed me in "Dad" Richey's hands for dedication as a six-month-old child.

The funeral was a graveside service in an old family cemetery outside of Hearne, a small town in central Texas, located in the middle of the triangle formed by Dallas/Fort Worth, Houston, and San Antonio. It was such a privilege for me to lead the service as we laid this gracious woman of God to rest beside her husband, my Uncle Louie. Aunt Ruby's life and testimony had never ceased to shape and mold my life. A great deal of preaching in the old days focused on heaven and hell, and I had always believed that, if there was anybody in the world who was going to heaven, it was my Aunt Ruby. She was a saint who not only talked about being a Christian, she lived like one too.

Chapter 13: Changing Times

❧☙

On April 29, 1996, we held a third Washington for Jesus rally on the National Mall with hundreds of thousands participating. But this time, we went to the actual steps of the Capitol Building, and every major Christian television network carried the event.

It was a day of miracles. In order to conduct a meeting on the Capitol steps, we had needed a "special use" permit that required unanimous approval by the entire U.S. Congress. In the weeks leading up to the event, two interns working on Capitol Hill learned of our need and chased down all the necessary signatures. These young interns had attended the 1980 Washington for Jesus rally as children.

Although it rained the day of the main event, keeping attendance down, thousands participated as Kenneth Hagin Jr., Jerry Falwell, Benny Hinn, Charles Green, Cindy Jacobs, Kim Clement, Bill Hamon, and many others prayed to overthrow the spiritual forces of darkness in the nation. The youth event the day before was a huge success with the crowd estimated at some 400,000.

Motivating a new generation were speakers like Ron Luce, Danny Chambers, Miles McPherson, Blaine Bartel, Kirk Pankratz, and many others. Musical guests included the Newsboys, Rebecca St. James, Kirk Franklin, Fred Hammond, Point of Grace, Christafari and a new band from Atlanta called Third Day. All of us came freely, offering our services to God with one simple vision—to pray for our nation to return to God!

Born to Preach

Each Washington event was a great blessing—and a great challenge. It seemed as if spiritual warfare would erupt afterwards and would invariably take its toll on John and me.

During the late 1990s, John and I faced some of the toughest challenges we had ever known as a married couple. But after a year of marital counseling and the prayers of close friends, we emerged from the trials with a greater love for each other and a stronger relationship than ever.

Although Rock Church had continued to grow, we didn't think that Costa Dier's prophecy from 25 years earlier—that we were "to build for the thousands"—had yet been completely achieved. But we had long since outgrown our round building.

Around this time, we received another prophetic word "to build again" because the Lord "had use of a new, larger facility." I felt God was calling us to become more than just a local church. We would prepare to host area-wide events for the entire Body of Christ, and point the way to greater unity among believers everywhere.

Since John was dealing with some difficult physical problems at the time, Robin and I decided we'd step into the gap and oversee the construction of the new sanctuary. However, John made an important contribution to the new building. He insisted that we place Bibles in different languages in the foundation of the building to symbolize that Rock Church had been founded on the Word of God.

By God's help and grace, the work was completed. In April 1997, a new church structure—valued in excess of $15 million and seating over 5,000—was dedicated with a week of celebration. Kenneth and Gloria Copeland, David Minor, and a host of ministers/friends came to help us celebrate what God had done with Rock Church.

Afterwards, it would not be long before that latest prophecy became a reality. Christian events planned for the Tidewater area seemed to gravitate to our new state-of-the-art facility. Beginning with Teen Mania's, Acquire the Fire, we soon hosted special meetings with Rod Parsley, Bishop T.D. Jakes, and Fred Hammond.

Joyce Meyer drew such huge crowds to the building that our overflow rooms filled to capacity, and we ultimately had to turn people away.

Recording artist Donnie McClurkin recorded the platinum-selling live album entitled *Psalms, Hymns, & Spiritual Songs* at Rock Church. Gospel singer Tye Tribbett came shortly afterwards to record his popular live album *Stand*. Truly, the Lord has used our new sanctuary in special ways and continues to do so.

On October 17, 1999, I was named Senior Pastor of the church, while John became Bishop over the Rock Ministerial Fellowship, our network of pastors and ministers. The Fellowship was now growing rapidly, with overseas missions in places like India, Africa, and South and Central America.

❧❧

Over the years, we had often wondered about a prophetic word that had been given to us during a convention at Coudersport. The prophecy stated that God was going to put property in our hands that would be developed into a "City of Refuge." It was to include a school, a church, a hospital, a radio station, and a Bible training center.

John had believed the prophecy and had come back to Virginia Beach and began looking for property. John and the elders settled on an 800-acre tract of land that backed up to the James River and purchased it. But we were not in one accord when he did.

I disagreed with John over what the prophecy had said and whether this particular tract of land was the right one. "The prophecy said you and I would hold hands, stand together and rejoice," I reminded him, "and that hasn't happened."

Problems arose immediately after the purchase, and the city repeatedly refused us any permits to utilize the land. "Well, it seems God is giving us another sign," John suggested.

The idea of a "City of Refuge" never left our hearts, but we had no idea how the prophetic word would be fulfilled. In the meanwhile, we kept the unused land.

For a number of years, John had been traveling to Liberia, and conducting services. In fact, when our nation was attacked by terrorists in New York City on September 11, 2001, he was in Liberia conducting revival services.

John had even organized a "Liberia for Jesus" rally that was attended by thousands, including a former President of the country. The event was credited by spiritual and political leaders as a pivotal point that unified the nation and subdued an imminent threat of takeover by Islamic militants.

Chapter 13: Changing Times

I had never accompanied him on his journeys to Liberia, but now John scheduled a trip there for both of us. In Monrovia, the capital city, we held meetings for several days in a rented building.

Later that week, we went out to look at forty acres that had been given to the Rock Church of Liberia. John and some others walked through the under-growth that covered much of the property, cutting brush with a machete as they went, until they reached the beach and the Atlantic Ocean. "This is gorgeous land," he remarked enthusiastically when he returned.

It was scorching hot, and I wanted to get back to the hotel in Monrovia, but we decided first to have a brief prayer. As I reached out to take John's hand, instantly I felt the presence of the Lord. "John," I said excitedly, "*this* is the City of Refuge...I *know* it."

"What?" he questioned, giving me a blank stare.

"I believe the Lord just told me this is the land for the City of Refuge—the property we've been looking for," I answered.

Although there was not a single building on the property at the time God spoke to me, I knew that would all change. We believed the prophetic word that had been given would be fulfilled. When God speaks prophetically, you can count on it!

In years to come, a church seating 2,500 people would be constructed, along with a school serving 1,000 students, a radio station broadcasting from dawn to dusk, and a free medical clinic. Babies were eventually born in the clinic; some of the boys were named "John" and some of the girls, "Anne".

Over the years, John shipped so many containers of supplies to our outreach in Liberia that I finally remarked, "You'd be sending Robin there if we hadn't nailed her down." John loved the Liberian people, and he was awed by what God was doing in the City of Refuge there.

Chapter 14

His Last Days

John Gimenez

Born to Preach

Chapter 14

His Last Days

"So when this corruptible has put on incorruption, and this mortal has put on immortality, then shall be brought to pass the saying that is written: 'Death is swallowed up in victory.'"

—*1 Corinthians 15:54 (NKJV)*

Our activities on a national level continued into the 21ˢᵗ century. In 2004, the Spirit of the Lord moved upon John again and he put out a call for a national prayer event, this time to reach Hispanic Christians.

The *America para Jesu Cristo* rally on the National Mall was planned for the fall instead of April because of permit issues. Although this event was first designed to be a Hispanic gathering, it began to grow and we ultimately decided to open the rally to everyone, naming it "America for Jesus".

Leaders such as Rod Parsley, Lou Engle, Ron Luce, Steve Munsey, Dennis & Ginger Lindsay, Stephen Strang, Rick Scarborough, and Donnie McClurkin joined us on the platform as speakers. Hispanic leaders like Alberto Motessi, Clark Ortiz,

Juan Boonstra, Adolfo Carrion, and many others led prayers for the nation.

Three years later, on April 29, 2007—on the 400th anniversary of the planting of the cross on the North American continent—we sponsored a renewed call to rededicate America to God. John commissioned our son-in-law, John Blanchard, to carry the vision forward calling the church in America to prayer and to renew this covenant.

The City of Virginia Beach officially approved a permit to set up a stage on the oceanfront only a short distance from where the original cross was planted by Robert Hunt centuries before.

The event, called "The Assembly 2007", brought together national leaders such as John Hagee, Kenneth and Gloria Copeland, Pat Robertson, Vonette Bright, Gordon Robertson, Wellington Boone, James Goll, Bill Hamon, Cindy Jacobs, Lou Engle, Harry Jackson, Marcus Lamb, Ron Luce, Billy Wilson, Hezekiah Walker, Ron Kenoly, and a host of other notables.

We planted several thousand crosses on the beachfront and prayed prayers of rededication. An Episcopal priest, representing descendants of the Anglican Church, washed the feet of Native American Chief Anne Richardson as an act of repentance and reconciliation. Pastor Custalow, a descendant from Pocahontas' tribe, presented a gift to Dr. Pat Robertson, himself related to Vicar Robert Hunt, expressing appreciation for the bringing of the Gospel to America.

On this historic day, others participated in rededication services throughout the nation. In Mississippi, over 500 crosses were planted alongside a major highway as a testimony to the

Chapter 14: His Last Days

Lordship of Christ over America. In California, an Anglican minister helped lead multiple churches in a cross planting ceremony. He ended with the same "Evensong" service that chaplain Robert Hunt had conducted for the newly arrived Jamestown settlers in 1607. In Oregon, churches led a "Reflection Service" to seek reconciliation with Native American groups mistreated in the past. In one city in Oklahoma, at exactly 4 p.m., over 200 church bells rang out honoring God for the day.

It was an amazing gathering and God moved in powerful ways among His people. Afterwards, John commented that he was glad to see that the mantle to call the church to prayer in America was evidently passing to the next generation.

But as we concluded the huge celebration, I was concerned. John's energy level was much lower than usual, and he was not feeling well. It was a disturbing sign of things to come.

❧❦

Our 40th wedding anniversary arrived on Saturday, September 1, 2007. To celebrate, we took a trip to Paris, France, that included a delightful river cruise with another couple. However, the whole time we were gone, John complained about his stomach. About a week after we returned home, he awoke in great pain about four o'clock in the morning.

"Anne, I've got to get something for this ache in my stomach," he said wearily. "I am *really* in pain."

A stomachache was all I thought the problem was, and I quickly called my son-in-law, asking him to take John to the emergency room at Norfolk General to get something for his discomfort.

I waited at home all morning, expecting him back at any moment. Then, shortly before noon, John Blanchard called me. "Sister Anne," he said, "I hate to tell you this but they're saying Brother John may have cancer!"

"*Cancer?* What are they talking about?" I said.

"One of the x-ray technicians just met with the doctor who told me the image on the film is consistent with cancer," he replied.

"How can an x-ray technician possibly know he has cancer?" I asked.

The hospital wanted to keep John for further evaluation. However, when I spoke with our family doctor, he recommended that we seek the help of some specialists. As a result, John soon checked out of the hospital, and several days later, went in for a colonoscopy.

After completing the test, the doctor came out to the waiting room and told me candidly, "He has cancer of the colon and it's in the fourth stage." It was now the middle of September; unfortunately, the specialist was not available to operate until the end of October.

The surgery was on a Tuesday, and for the next few days, Robin and I spent night and day with John. At seven a.m. Friday, I got a call from the doctor. "You need to come to the hospital immediately," he instructed me. "Get someone to drive you."

I called Robin, and she drove me to the hospital, where the doctor informed me that John's heart had gone down to 23% of function. The team of doctors who were working on John finally decided to put him "under"—to medically induce a coma—because he was in such pain.

Seven days later, the team decided to take him off the respirator and bring him back to consciousness. Amazingly, John started breathing on his own even though he was only semi-conscious for days.

For the next two weeks, I went to the hospital every day. Each Sunday morning I was there checking on John before heading to church to preach. It was always a shock to see him. With a sheet draped over his body and tubes running everywhere, he seemed only half-alive, and I'd stand beside his bed weeping and praying until I had to leave to preach.

When John had been in the hospital for over three weeks, I began to sense he needed some advanced treatment. On the Tuesday before Thanksgiving, after much consideration and prayer, we took him to the Burzynski Clinic in Houston. We remained there for some three weeks while John was being treated.

The doctors didn't want to be overly optimistic, but they kept assuring us that he was responding well to their prescribed treatment regimen. Unfortunately, he was still losing weight, and by the time we returned to Virginia, he weighed only 135 pounds.

But John had always been a survivor. During his New York City days, he had been hit by a taxi, he had been shot, and he had fallen off a roof several stories high. In addition, in 1988, he had nearly died during surgery. God had sustained him in all these things, and I fully expected He was going to raise him up from this sickbed as well.

Standing beside his bed one morning, I declared aloud, "John Gimenez, if I can help it, I won't let you die…I simply won't let that happen." I followed the instructions the doctors had given us in Houston "to the letter." I believed if I did that—with God's help—John would recover.

I got up at five o'clock every morning and gave him his first dose of pills for the day. He had to wait an hour before he could eat, and then every two hours, he got more pills.

"His body is quite amazing," one doctor told me. "His immune system shouldn't even be working now, but there is no cancer in his brain, bones, kidneys or liver."

After we returned to Virginia Beach, we continued his endless series of medications and had regular check-ups with his local doctors. I only left home to take him to the doctor and to come to church on Sunday to conduct services. We were to fly back to Houston for a clinic appointment six weeks later.

In early December, John's long-time friend, Bishop Val Melendez, suddenly passed away after a brief but valiant battle with pancreatic cancer. Val was another native New Yorker of Puerto Rican heritage; like John, he was pastoring a church in the South. His death was a crushing blow for John.

I had planned to attend the funeral in Ahoskie, N.C., and read a Scripture, but John said no. Uncharacteristically, he insisted on sending a personal letter and dictated a beautiful remembrance of his dear friend to be read at the funeral.

For weeks, I could tell John was going downhill physically by simply looking at him. But I refused to pay attention to what I saw because I simply believed he was going to get better.

Chapter 14: His Last Days

Somehow I just believed God would intervene and John would come out of this battle.

January 2008 quickly turned into February. On Thursday and Friday, February 7th and 8th, John refused his medicine. I thought to myself, *He's just tired of taking eight pills every two hours.* But he refused the medication on Saturday and Sunday as well.

On Monday night, John Blanchard heard him talk all night long in his sleep. He seemed to be conversing with two other people in the room, glancing from one to the other. My son-in-law later recalled that this reminded him of how Bishop John shared that he had been visited by two angels four months earlier following surgery. John Blanchard said that he felt this conversation was preparation for my husband's journey to heaven.

Tuesday, John had a morning appointment with his doctor. That morning I gave him a sponge bath, dressed him, combed his hair, and looked into his dark brown eyes. "I love you," I whispered to him.

His response was identical: "I love you." Those were the last words we would ever speak to each other on planet earth.

Ray Strickland, one of the staff pastors, and John Blanchard drove John to his appointment. About four o'clock on February 12th, the phone rang. John had had a massive stroke. The doctor wanted me to bring him home and make him comfortable. "You could put him in the hospital but he probably won't live another twenty-four hours," he explained.

John Blanchard had already returned home, but he too received a phone call about John's stroke. He and Robin met me at the house to discuss what we should do. Based on the doctor's advice that we bring John home and surround him with family and friends, John Blanchard began to head for the doctor's office.

But just as he was leaving, his cell phone rang. He told Robin what the doctor explained on the phone line. Her daddy was gone. He had been listening to one of his own songs, "I Had a Talk with God Last Night," on his iPod when he closed his eyes, breathed his last, and stepped into the presence of God.

I had just called Pat Robertson and was telling him about John's stroke. Just then, Robin burst into the room, saying, "Mom…Mom…the doctor's office just called back…Dad's gone…Dad's gone!"

On the Sunday before, I had told Robin that it looked as if I would survive her father. "But when God takes him," I promised, "you and I will shout him through the gates of glory."

"Shout with me, Robin," I said with tears running down my cheeks. "God, your servant John's coming home…receive him… oh Lord!" I heard my words ringing in my heart as we shouted him through the gates.

We wept and shouted until we were hoarse. I knew John had gone home in victory. It seems whenever any of us is faced with death we fight, kick, and punch, resisting to the very last breath. Then, when God speaks in the depths of our being, *Come,* we drop everything constraining us and leap through the door to receive the crown of life. That's exactly what John did.

Chapter 14: His Last Days

❧❧

Several days later, at his celebration service, I heard the voice of the Lord as I sat staring at John's casket. *I took him,* said God's Spirit to my heart.

I knew it was true.

One of his local doctors had predicted John would die gasping for breath. That didn't happen; his lungs remained perfectly clear. And he didn't expire from cancer, either—every test showed his body clear and responding to treatment. The answer was simple. God took him home.

Robin had asked about the flowers for the top of the casket. I said red roses.

"Red roses?" she asked.

"Robin, your father never gave me any other kind of flowers but red roses," I answered.

Rock Church was filled to capacity, with thousands attending John's memorial service. Pat Robertson spoke from the depths of his heart about "my dear friend," John Gimenez.

John's testimony was printed on our memorial program, and Pat read the testimonial with compassion and grace. John had been a former drug addict who rose above his past and with God's help accomplished great things for His kingdom. He was a man who touched thousands of lives.

Bishop Courtney McBath reminisced that John "had set the bar high for every minister in this area. He took the brunt of having a woman stand by his side in the ministry. Today, we call it team ministry…but John faced the critics with what he believed."

Then, Brother Minor stepped to the podium. "I never thought I would ever bury John," he said softly. "I always thought he would bury me."

Few men knew John as David Minor had. He spoke from a heart of brokenness and enduring love for the gift of this man, John Gimenez.

As he concluded his remarks, Brother Minor said, "I asked God, 'What could I possibly say to Sister Anne in light of her loss?' And He said, 'Run, Anne. Run.' That's what God's saying.

"Then I asked God, what would John want to say to Anne?" he continued. "He said 'I will meet you at the Eastern Gate with a bouquet of red roses.'"

I knew it was God talking because Brother Minor had not seen the casket and could not have known that I had chosen red roses for it because John had always given me red roses.

At the graveside, Brother Minor spoke briefly about the changing of seasons. "The rain will fall, the leaves will turn, the snow will cover this ground as seasons come and go..."

And then, the moment I had dreaded finally came—I had to walk away from the casket at the graveside. No one had ever told me how hard that would be. It took a gut-wrenching effort to walk away and turn my back on John's coffin.

The finality was overwhelming. "Oh, God, come in this moment," I prayed.

Chapter 15

Waters to Swim In

*Ordained Bishop
of the RMF*

Born to Preach

Chapter 15

Waters to Swim In

"Afterward he measured a thousand; and it was a river that I could not pass over: for the waters were risen, waters to swim in...."

—*Ezekiel 47:5 (KJV)*

My world changed overnight with John's abrupt passing. We had been inseparable in forty years of marriage. I could hardly imagine my life apart from him.

Yet, I had known when he became ill that he didn't have a long life ahead; I simply never thought he'd go *that* quickly. It had been a mere four months since the unexpected diagnosis of cancer. I had thought we had perhaps another year or two together. Now the suddenness of his death stunned me as I rehearsed in my thoughts what had happened.

"He was there one moment," one of the nurses explained later, "and the next he was gone. There was no struggle, no sound, no gasping for breath. He was just gone."

The doctor concluded that John had suffered a massive stroke.

The next few days had passed in a blur. The wake. The funeral. The church filled with thousands of friends—people who had been touched by John's life. It seemed so many people—from janitors to television preachers—all considered the unassuming John Gimenez to be their special friend.

I was in a state of near collapse. I'd actually had to pray for the strength to take part in the services. Some may have thought I looked okay considering the depth of my loss, but emotionally, I was in a state of unending shock.

Several weeks later, Robin wanted me to take a cruise somewhere to rest. But I had something different in mind. "I just have to go home," I told her.

By this time in my life, my mother and father, as well as my only sister had passed away…and now, John. Somehow, I just wanted to go home and "touch base." I didn't know exactly what that would involve, just that I needed to reconnect with my roots.

Perhaps my feeling was something like Jacob's in the Old Testament when he went back to a place called Bethel (Genesis 35). Jacob worshiped God at the very spot where he had met Him many years before. Maybe that's what I was looking to do with my trip back to Texas.

With my granddaughter Amelia (who was now 15) as my traveling companion, I flew to Corpus Christi, Texas—"the sparkling city by the sea" as the radio stations once called it. I had forgotten the feelings I had for Corpus; it was such a beautiful town to have grown up in on the south Texas coast.

Amelia and I took a hotel room down at the oceanfront and spent several days visiting my old childhood haunts—the house where my parents raised me at 813 Anderson Street, the high school I attended, the church on Elizabeth and Alameda Streets that groomed me for ministry. They were all so much smaller in size than I remembered.

But for sure, most of my memories of growing up were rooted in that place. It had been my home from the age of fourteen until I was over thirty. Perhaps I needed to touch the past as I considered what the future held for me.

With John's sudden "homegoing", the under-pinnings of my life had been shaken to the core. Corpus Christi was where God had first called me as a teenager. Now that I was about to embark on a new phase of life and ministry without John, it helped to remember that God had used me as a single woman before. I knew I could draw strength from that fact.

Then, Amelia and I left Corpus Christi for San Antonio, traveling I-37 across the Nueces River to the northwest and the rural areas of Mathis and Lake Corpus Christi. I wanted to show her the burgeoning city of San Antonio with its beautiful River Walk and the historic Alamo. In addition, I wanted to introduce her to some of the friends and churches that had shaped my life in the past.

As I drove, I knew what John would have said about my road trip—"That's typically Anne." As a single woman and a preacher, I had driven from Texas to most of my church services in other states, from Illinois to Connecticut, and even Canada.

And when things got stressful at Rock Church, where John and I pastored, my diversion of choice was to get in the car and drive somewhere.

But all of that was now in the past.

After returning from my trip with Amelia, on May 8, 2008, I was consecrated as Bishop over the Rock Ministerial Fellowship, succeeding my husband. The day had been declared "Anne Gimenez Day" by the mayor of Virginia Beach. Our entire team of pastors throughout RMF in the States and overseas was on hand for the occasion.

I had actually struggled over the prospect of being installed as a female bishop over the Fellowship, even though I knew it was my rightful place as successor to my husband.

At the consecration event, Bishop Courtney McBath of Calvary Revival Church in Norfolk observed: "When they looked for the best man for the job," he said with a smile, "it turned out to be...*a woman!*"

⚘

When the time came for the Bishop's medallion to be placed around my neck—the very one John had used—I felt something unusual. For the first time since his passing, I sensed John's presence. It was something like an electric shock, and my tears began to flow.

It was as if John were placing the medallion upon me himself, with complete approval. A new and different anointing came upon my life that night. Its electric suddenness was palpable, and made me catch my breath.

It was then that I shared my vision for the John Gimenez School of International Ministry that would train students to be missionaries throughout the world. "I know this will be the proper and fitting way to remember John," I told the people.

Chapter 15: Waters to Swim In

The anointing that came upon me that night was a sovereign impartation from God to handle the job that has been entrusted to me for this season of my life. I felt as if I were entering "waters to swim in," as Ezekiel prophesied in the Old Testament (Ezekiel 47:12).

I first got my feet wet in these waters when I was in the church in Corpus Christi. Later, the waters were at my knees when I did evangelistic work, and they came up to my waist during the pastorate in Virginia Beach. And now, they had become waters to swim in.

I no longer struggle as I did in the past to be accepted as a woman in ministry. I no longer wonder whether I'll be asked back to preach. I'm free now to minister and do the will of God—going where He wants me to go. It's a freedom I've walked in ever since I first met and married John Gimenez.

Within two months of becoming Bishop, I made overseas trips to visit our churches in the Ivory Coast and Liberia. In 2009, I traveled again to Liberia and then to Fiji, the last place John visited. He told me it was the most beautiful place he had ever seen—and I agreed.

The Rock Ministerial Fellowship, our network of churches and evangelists, is growing throughout the world, and I will be off soon to visit affiliated churches in India.

As I contemplate what God has done, I recall a prophecy given by Bishop David Huskins at a recent RMF conference:

Daughter, in this hour, you shall see the fruit of your labor, you shall see the ingathering of your harvest and you shall know that your labor has not been in vain.

Born to Preach

For I was not just using you for that day, I was preparing you for this day. It is for this day you were born and it is for this day you will see your greatest harvest for I, the Lord thy God, shall release a new harvest, a new season, a new freedom, and a new liberty to you and through you...

❧❦

One of the most important things I have realized through my life of ministry is that God gave me the ability in my Spirit to hear God. That is what has led and directed me; that's how I preach; that's how I live my life; that's how I pastor the church.

I have to hear from God, and when I do, I am not going to change my direction.

I have found that everything I preach comes around to this: faith comes by hearing, and hearing by the Word of God (Romans 10:17).

Seek God until you know you've heard a word from Heaven; when you have heard, hold on to that with all of your heart. That is how I have always known that I was born to preach. It has been my life! Praise the Living God.

Epilogue

Miracle Sunday: The first Sunday
back in the pulpit after illness

Born to Preach

Epilogue

Just as the finishing touches were being applied to Anne Gimenez's inspiring story, an entirely different and ominous scenario encircled her life and almost prematurely took her to heaven.

It all began in January 2010, during an ocean cruise with members of the Rock Ministerial Fellowship. For some six weeks prior, she had been battling a blood platelet disorder, but her health had improved so much that her physician had cleared her to make this winter voyage.

Yet, instead of the trip being enjoyable, Anne was ill for most of it. By the time she and Robin returned to Ft. Lauderdale, she was unable to fly back home and ultimately was rushed to a local hospital, where doctors predicted the worst. "She may not make it," several physicians told Robin.

Robin texted the desperate news to her husband, John Blanchard, who was in the midst of a Sunday morning service in Virginia Beach. John immediately stopped the service and called for prayer. Instantly, the congregation was crying out with heartfelt prayers on behalf of their pastor.

In quick succession, Anne suffered major organ failures—heart, lungs, kidneys. For some eighteen days, she was on life support, existing in the haze of a medically-induced coma.

When she finally awoke from the darkness, she believed she was paralyzed. Other than being able to turn her head, she could move no part of her body. Robin constantly resisted suggestions by well-meaning hospital staff that her mother still might die, or, if she should survive, she'd probably wind up in a nursing home.

After some three weeks in a Florida hospital, doctors there were still unable to determine the cause of Anne's illness. Frustrated, Robin knew there was an answer somewhere and contacted a friend in Dallas, Texas, who knew some key physicians at Presbyterian Hospital.

On the second anniversary of John Gimenez's homegoing, Anne was flown to Dallas, landing in the midst of a terrible snowstorm. Once admitted to Presbyterian, she immediately began a regimen of physical therapy and further tests to pinpoint the mysterious illness. Along the way, she battled pneumonia and the rigors of physical therapy to gain the ability to walk again.

Ultimately, Anne was released from the hospital and admitted to a new facility that specialized in rehabilitation. There, she made giant strides, going from a wheelchair to a walker to actually being able to walk freely.

Expecting to be released from treatment and return home, Anne began making the rounds of all her doctors for final approval and release. One of the doctors insisted that a particular medication for blood pressure required *two* pills a day. Until then, the hospital had suspended the use of this medication because her blood pressure had normalized; but on this doctor's advice, she promptly began taking it.

Within three days, Anne was in a medicated haze, unable to get out of bed or function in any meaningful way. Robin rushed her back for tests with another cardiologist, who immediately determined that Anne had been overdosed on the blood pressure medication.

"She should have been taking one pill a day," he explained, "not two. If she had continued with the double dose, she would not have awakened after another day or so."

Finally, an infectious disease specialist diagnosed her overall problem as a virus that had attacked her heart—*viral myocarditis*. Its symptoms are similar to those of a heart attack, except that coronary arteries aren't blocked.

This viral myocarditis—often caused by common viruses—had been a tool of the enemy meant to take Anne's life prematurely. But God stepped in and spared her life—thanks to the fervent prayers of the Body of Christ and the persistent determination of her daughter, Robin!

In late April 2010, Anne flew back home to Virginia Beach after being away almost 14 weeks. On July 4th—Independence Day—she returned to the pulpit to preach for the first time since becoming ill. The congregation greeted her with a thunderous round of applause and shouts of rejoicing.

Photographs of Anne in the pulpit that day show a distinctive aura of lights throughout the building and a glorious brilliance on her face.

Born to Preach

All of heaven appeared to be rejoicing at Anne Gimenez's return to the pulpit and the wonderful renewal of the calling of God upon her life.

Without question, Anne believes her life has been spared so that she might "lay hands" upon another generation of God's servants and send them forth to the ends of the earth to proclaim the glorious Gospel of the Lord Jesus.

Amen.

Afterword

Rock Church, as well as my life and ministry, has always been an outright miracle of God.

Through the years, many people asked John and me, "What is the secret of Rock Church's success?" Invariably, we would answer, "We don't know!" After all, we had no business plan or special strategy mapped out to ensure the success of the ministry.

Looking back, however, I believe the "secret" was that John and I only moved when we heard a clear word from the Lord—"a rhema."

A _rhema_ is defined as a word that is spoken, an utterance. It is in contrast to *logos*, which is the written expression of a thought, a message, a discourse. In Matthew 4:4, where Jesus quotes Deuteronomy 8:3, He uses this Greek word _rhema_: "…Man shall not live by bread alone, but by every <u>word</u> that proceeds from the mouth of God" (NKJV).

Some call rhema "a heard word." John and I always believed that faith comes by hearing a *rhema* from heaven.

Everything we did, everything we built, was because we first heard the word of the Lord in our hearts. It never mattered what the expense would be or what it required of us. If God said it, we would immediately start out to accomplish it, and God blessed our obedience from the very beginning.

Now, a new day has dawned, bringing with it new challenges and great possibilities. I have received a fresh word from heaven—a *rhema*—with an exciting new vision for launching the John Gimenez School of International Ministry.

Already, we are making preparation to inaugurate this school to train young men and women—called to the ministry—just as John and I were summoned to go throughout the world and preach the Gospel.

If you or someone you know is interested in just such a school of International Ministry—where students will be taught the dynamics of touching lives for the Lord Jesus, you can write or call our office today for an application. It could be one of the most important decisions you will ever make.

About the Co-author...

ROBERT PAUL LAMB has worn a number of hats since entering the ministry in 1972, including author, pastor, evangelist, prophet, preacher of the Gospel, and missionary. However, he is best known for having authored more than forty-five books (with over four million copies in print), many of which were written on the lives of extraordinary men and women of God.

Marking Your Children for God

A must for parents, expectant parents, grandparents, aunts or uncles – It's never too early and it's never too late! A collection of sermons by Anne Gimenez.

Beyond Tradition

Dr. Anne Gimenez explains the true meaning of the celebrations of Easter, Passover, and the Lord's Supper.

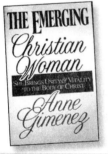

The Emerging Christian Woman

Anne Gimenez speaks to us from her heart, bringing an honest, personal account of some of the frustrations of life as a Christian woman in today's world and how she found victory in Christ through every challenge.

Upon This Rock

The fascinating story of how God took two people of incredibly different backgrounds. He was an ex-drug addict; she, a woman preacher. But once united in marriage they were shaped into one of the most effective husband/wife ministry teams.

PRAYER OF SALVATION

God loves you—no matter who you are, no matter what your past. God loves you so much that He gave His one and only begotten Son for you. The Bible tells us that "...whoever believes in him shall not perish but have eternal life" (John 3:16 NIV). Jesus laid down His life and rose again so that we could spend eternity with Him in heaven and experience His absolute best on earth. If you would like to receive Jesus into your life, say the following prayer out loud and mean it from your heart.

Heavenly Father, I come to You admitting that I am a sinner. Right now, I choose to turn away from sin, and I ask You to cleanse me of all unrighteousness. I believe that Your Son, Jesus, died on the cross to take away my sins. I also believe that He rose again from the dead so that I might be forgiven of my sins and made righteous through faith in Him. I call upon the name of Jesus Christ to be the Savior and Lord of my life. Jesus, I choose to follow You and ask that You fill me with the power of the Holy Spirit. I declare that right now I am a child of God. I am free from sin and full of the righteousness of God. I am saved in Jesus' name. Amen.

If you prayed this prayer to receive Jesus Christ as your Savior for the first time, please contact us on the Web at **www.harrisonhouse.com** to receive a free book.

Or you may write to us at

Harrison House • P.O. Box 35035 • Tulsa, Oklahoma 74153